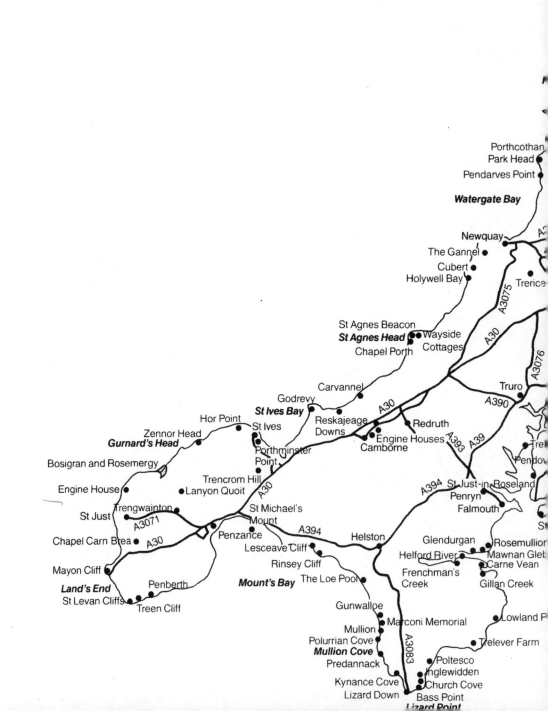

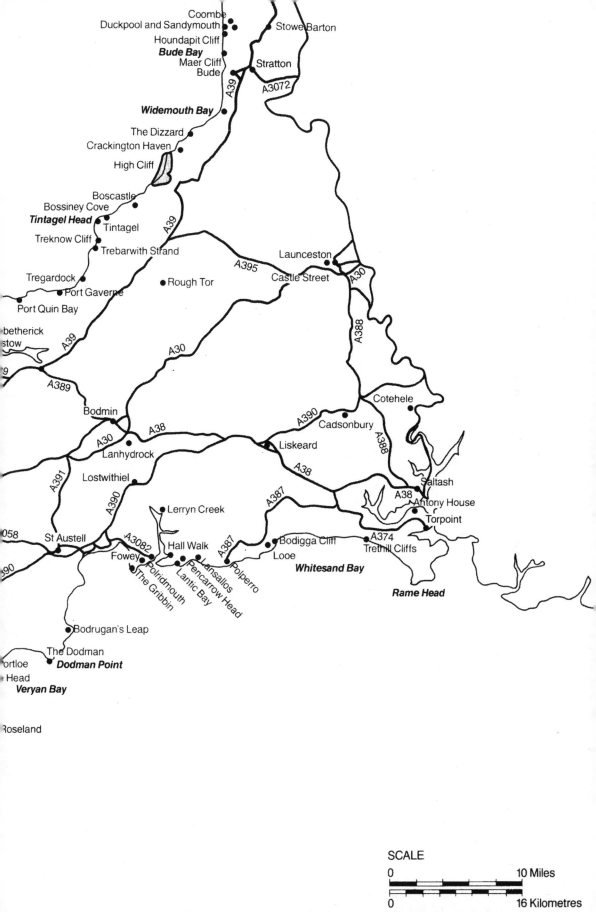

Coombe
Duckpool and Sandymouth
Houndapit Cliff
Bude Bay
Maer Cliff
Bude
Stowe Barton
Stratton
A39
A3072

Widemouth Bay

The Dizzard
Crackington Haven

High Cliff

Boscastle
Bossiney Cove
Tintagel Head
Tintagel
Treknow Cliff
Trebarwith Strand
A39

Launceston
Castle Street
A395
A30

Tregardock
Port Gaverne
Rough Tor
A388

Port Quin Bay

betherick
stow
A39

9
A389

A30
A38
Bodmin
A30
Lanhydrock

A391
Lostwithiel
A390
A30

Cotehele
Cadsonbury
A390
A388

Liskeard
A38

Saltash
A38
Antony House
Torpoint

058
St Austell
A3082
Lerryn Creek
Hall Walk
A387
Bodigga Cliff
Looe
A374
Trethill Cliffs

390
Fowey
Polridmouth
The Gribbin
Lansallos
Pencarrow Head
Lantic Bay
A387
Polperro
Whitesand Bay

Rame Head

Bodrugan's Leap
The Dodman
ortloe
Dodman Point
Head
Veryan Bay

Roseland

SCALE

0   10 Miles

0   16 Kilometres
● National Trust Properties

NATIONAL TRUST HISTORIES

CORNWALL

JACK RAVENSDALE

Series Editor Richard Muir

RETRO CLASSICS
is a collection of facsimile reproductions
of popular titles from the 1980s and 1990s

National Trust Histories: Cornwall
was first published in 1984
by William Collins & Co Ltd.

Re-issued in 2015 as a Retro Classic
by G2 Entertainment
in association with Lennard Publishing
Windmill Cottage
Mackerye End
Harpenden
Hertfordshire
AL5 5DR

Copyright © 1984 J R Ravensdal and Lennard Books Ltf

ISBN 978-1-78281-147-3

Editor: Michael Leitch
Designed by David Pocknell's Company Ltd

Printed and bound by Halstan uk

This book is a facsimile reproduction of *Cornwall*
as it was originally published in 1984.
No attempt has been made to alter any of the wording
with the benefit of hindsight, or to update the book in any way.

CONTENTS

EDITOR'S INTRODUCTION

One can holiday in a seaside resort in Cornwall and yet learn no more about the Cornish and their land than the package-tripper to Benidorm finds out about Spain. Newquay and Penzance can be welcome havens at the end of a long – for many, a surprisingly long – journey, but just beyond the resorts there is a countryside of rugged beauty which is packed with interest and historical details and is still, in most places, reasonably unspoilt.

Cornwall has its own language, culture and outlook and a powerful individuality; its scenery is unique in Britain, and to see a remotely similar countryside one must travel across the sea to another Celtic bastion, Brittany. It is also a place where reality is far more fascinating and diverse than the popular perceptions suggest. Hidden coves, where smugglers and wreckers lurked, and dubious Arthurian fantasies tend to dominate the visions of outsiders or 'up-country' folk, and while the coastline is the equal of any and the folklore as rich and unlikely as can be, the real Cornish landscape and history have been strangely neglected by the public in general.

Although its terrain is relatively gentle, Cornwall is indisputably a part of upland Britain – a land of damp and rather impoverished soils, offering only the most modest returns for the farmer's hard labour: a place where mining and quarrying have, for all their dangers, lured many toilers from the land. Cornwall offers the visitor a remarkable portfolio of monuments. The prehistoric legacy of small tombs and circles could scarcely be surpassed, and if the Roman endowment is meagre, there are some tough little medieval castles, a few quite exceptional mansions and a most remarkable heritage of industrial relics.

Jack Ravensdale has provided a colourful but authoritative account of the Cornwall which the holidaymaker so often misses. His work as a historian and as author of the scholarly study of a group of Fen-edge villages, *Liable to Floods,* has won him the esteem of many professional historians. But Jack is a most modest person, and, although he has been a good friend since we worked together on some photographs for his best-seller, *History On Your Doorstep,* it took a special call to extract brief biographical details. After completing his degree at Cambridge University, he became an adult education tutor with the WEA, covering north and mid Cornwall and living in Wadebridge and Minions. In the course of those seven years he developed a close understanding of the creation of the Cornish landscape and he maintains his contacts with the area in the course of periodic visits to his numerous Cornish cousins. On leaving Cornwall he taught in Cambridgeshire, becoming Principal Lecturer in the History of the English Landscape at Homerton College and receiving a doctorate in 1972 from the University of Leicester where he had been working part-time in the Department of English Local History. In 1981 he retired from teaching in order to develop an expanding career as a writer.

Richard Muir
Great Shelford, 1983

THE ENDOWMENT

Cornwall was bound to be different: its rocks had made it so. They are of several kinds and have different origins, but it is the grey granite which dominates Cornwall's landscapes and moods.

The story of the rocks began around 400–300 million years ago, in the Devonian and Carboniferous periods, when the land that is now Cornwall lay beneath a sea. Sediments deposited in this sea accumulated to produce the Devonian shales and limestones of north Cornwall and Devon and the Carboniferous sandstones and mudstones which form the greater part of the surface geology of Cornwall. At the end of the Carboniferous period, around 290 million years ago, great earth movements centred further south in Europe thrust an enormous mass of molten rock or 'magma' from far below the surface of the earth into the zones underlying the Cornish landscape. The sedimentary rocks above were bulged upwards, and wherever they came into close contact with the searing magma they were scorched and changed or 'metamorphosed'.

The magma cooled and solidified to form a great underground mass or 'batholith' of granite, which originally lay about 8 miles (12km) below the surface. In the course of the subsequent millennia, erosion has stripped away the rocks covering the higher domes or 'cupolas' of the batholith, and the granite has been exposed to form the distinctive moorstone landscapes of the Scilly Isles, Land's End, Carnmenellis, St Austell, Bodmin Moor and, in Devon, Dartmoor. Masses of rotted granite, decomposed by scalding waters released by the cooling magma, form the white kaolinite or china clay deposits which are quarried at the domes of the granite outcrops where the water was vented. No well-sited

Above: Cliffs at Bosigran. Granite outcrops such as this display a clear system of joints, and the cracks seem to have opened as a result of the release of pressure when erosion removed the heavy overburden of rock.

Below: Rough Tor, on Bodmin Moor, is the second highest Cornish tor and looks over a remarkable concentration of hut circles and compounds from the Bronze Age, and field systems dating from every period since then.

china clay pit has ever reached the bottom of the deposit, and the finest-quality Cornish clays are unequalled elsewhere in the world. When Cornwall arose from the ocean the good fairies were unusually active.

Different rocks are found at the Lizard, where a great thrust has forced up serpentine, gabbros and schists. These varied rocks have long been valued by man and were exploited in prehistoric times by the makers of prestigious greenstone axes; since they weather into valuable and distinctive clays, they have also been exploited by potters for thousands of years.

As the granite cooled, fissures developed where the rocks shrank and cracked, mostly in or near the 'metamorphic aureole' or changed zone. Many but not all of these fissures ran east and west, and when they received new mineral-bearing igneous rocks from below, they shaped the lodes of ore that crystallized inside them. This process happened more than once, and was complicated by fractures and earth movement, until the prediction of where rich veins were and would lead, turned mining into a gambler's hazard where both riches and poverty were to be found, but with not much in between.

Emergence and submergence of the whole peninsula occurred from time to time, and this helped to weather the granite a little, but planed away the softer surrounding rocks to leave raised beaches and flat platforms between the moors and the coast. So the county was slowly shaped for mining and farming, and where the sea cut in to join the river valleys, havens (if often small and dangerous to approach) made possible the exploitation of the enormous length of the Cornish coastline by fishermen.

Ancient Cornwall

'Old Men's Workings' is how the Cornish miner labelled the earthworks, shafts and tunnels left by the tinners of past centuries. Now all Cornwall seems like old men's workings. Our first task here is to set aside these comparatively recent remains and examine the handiwork of the ancient Cornishmen.

Fifty years ago, the archaeologist tended to explain every change in pottery style by the advent of conquering strangers, who invaded and drove out or massacred their predecessors. Now, with the aid of modern sciences, a new and more subtle picture is emerging. At one time we detect emigration, at another immigration; trading contacts, or systems of gifts and exchange. The South-West may import or imitate, may move parallel to or follow, but on some occasions it can lead. Central to the development of the new knowledge of prehistoric Cornwall has been the work of Professor Charles Thomas at Gwithian in the far west of the county. There a series of sand-blows had sealed successive layers and the archaeologist was able to uncover typical sites for most periods of Cornish prehistory.

Professor Thomas even found a site at Gwithian from the Paleolithic (Old Stone) Age before 8000 BC, which had been represented scarcely at all before in Cornish finds. When H. O'N. Hencken wrote his remarkable *Archaeology of Cornwall and Scilly* in the Thirties, the only Paleolithic axe which he could record as found in the county was an imported one, brought into the area by an outsider.

The Mesolithic Beginnings

Coastal sites from the Mesolithic (Middle Stone) Age are paralleled by those of similar cultures which run right down the Atlantic coasts of Europe and Africa. Most but not all of the Cornish sites linked to this period have been coastal. In the absence here of high-quality flint the natives used beach pebbles. Where they carried the pebbles up to their 'knapping' floor on the cliff top, they left thousands of small flakes and cores, discarded once the minute artefacts so much used by this culture had been struck. On the headland at Trevelgue, just along the coast from Newquay, every wild storm at one time picked clean a few more such flints where the turf was broken and the soil was thin. Finding them was easy as most had acquired a white patina with time. Such Mesolithic flint workings were quite common, and many more must await discovery; others have vanished into the sea as the cliffs were eroded.

At Trevelgue these first inhabitants left behind middens which suggest that a large part of their diet was stew made from pounded-up shell-fish, which they ate complete, shells and all. Although there were remains of other foods, such as bird and small animal bones, these were relatively few, and the general impression conveyed by the middens is one of dire poverty. However, other inland and upland Mesolithic sites tell a rather different tale.

On the high moor, in the sandy margins of Dozmary Pool (near Jamaica Inn), a profusion of microliths from this period has been found, alongside later Neolithic and Bronze Age arrowheads, variously leaf-shaped, and tanged and barbed. Particularly plentiful are the *petit tranchet* arrowheads with blunt, chisel-like tips designed for hunting birds. Similar Mesolithic finds have been reported at Crowdy Marsh on Davidstow Moor. These sites, with their opportunities for fishing and fowling, would have offered a better living than coastal beachcombing. It has recently been suggested that these contrasting Mesolithic sites do not represent the different ways of life of rival cultures, but seasonal shifts in annual cycles as communities migrated, cropping in turn the produce of the upland heaths, meres and marshes, and the resources of the sea, lowlands and forest. Much of the evidence which might have illuminated Mesolithic life has disappeared, not only into the sea, but also under the blanket bog which later grew over so many potential upland sites.

Elsewhere in southern Britain, recent evidence suggests that the first attempts at animal husbandry in England came in the Mesolithic period rather than later in the Neolithic, as was previously thought. The Mesolithic now appears as the period when Cornwall first acquired reasonable numbers of human inhabitants. The seasonality of the lives of birds and beasts, of fish and plants, would have imposed a seasonal rhythm on the lives of human beings who came to exploit and control them. The burnt peat and charcoal found in the Dozmary Pool region could, for instance, represent deliberate land clearance for the benefit of browsing animals, possibly an early stage in the development from hunting to pastoral life-styles.

Annual cycles of nomadic life often include seasonal visits to inter-tribal meeting-places. There, among other activities exchanges of goods take place. Petrologists, who study and classify rocks, have identified the movement of stone and stone implements over Britain and even beyond as a feature of the Neolithic period, but new evidence suggests that something of the sort had already begun in the Mesolithic. It looks as if the later period owes something to the earlier in the way that social patterns developed. Certainly, the exchange of implements continued and expanded. On the other hand, some groups seem to have continued Mesolithic styles of hunting, fishing and gathering while living alongside the Neolithic farming communities.

The New Stone Age

In Britain as a whole, the mixed farming way of life which marks the arrival of the Neolithic period may have been introduced as early as 5000 BC. One of the most important Neolithic settlements that has so far been investigated in Cornwall is on Carn Brea above Redruth. Carbon-14 dating has shown very early activity indeed. Near the summit there is a massive dry stone wall from the Neolithic period, built over a hut which itself was built over land cleared for cultivation prior to about 3800 BC. The artefacts – pottery, flint implements, and a saddle quern used for grinding flour – firmly identify this part of the site as belonging to grain-growing farmers of the New Stone Age. Elsewhere in England, hilltop 'causewayed enclosures' with earthen ramparts and interrupted ditches were being built. More common than these sites are the 'open' ones which show up merely as flint scatters on ploughed land. Gwithian has one such site which lay in an environment produced by forest clearance at some stage in the Neolithic period.

Early Neolithic artefacts, where they are novel, reflect the changes from the previous cultures. Farming implies settlement, and the flint scatters sometimes suggest continuity in the use of places from the Mesolithic right through to the early Bronze Age. Leaf-shaped arrowheads suggest a survival of some hunting alongside the new farming although at least one example had been used to kill a man. Seed-time and harvest imply the storage of grain, and round-bottomed jars and storage pits are found upon virtually every site of this period. The polished flint and other stone axes have been shown to be efficient for forest clearance, and these are the artefacts which define the Neolithic as an age of expanding agriculture. Some of them seem to have been used as hoes and reinforcements to the points of primitive ploughs or 'ards'.

When Roger Mercer excavated some Bronze Age huts on Stannon Down, Bodmin Moor, he found a layer of cultivated soil and a field system under some of the huts. In this layer he found two polished greenstone implements, one of them sealed in the cultivated layer by the wall of a hut built over it. There was no sign of forest clearance, and the context of these implements suggests that, whether as hoes or as plough points, they were the tools which produced the fields of little strips running down the hillside.

The petrological analysis of the crystalline structure of axes has enabled about a dozen Cornish localities to be identified as the places of origin of polished greenstone implements found over most of Britain, especially in Wessex. One of these sources is now out under the sea in Mount's Bay. It was submerged when the sea drowned the homes and fields which begin to emerge again at very low tides between Scilly and the mainland.

The distance at which some of these axes have been found from their places of origin indicates a network of trade throughout southern Britain and reaching out beyond. It is very likely that there were small trading communities in walled hilltop settlements like Carn Brea. Imports into the South-West, which at least partly balanced the export of polished greenstone axes, include axes of polished flint brought from the flint mines of Sussex and Norfolk. This exchange seems to have gone on for two millennia.

Something of this trade can be discovered through the scientific study of the pastes of Neolithic pottery. The 'gabbroic' clays of the Lizard Pensinsula are quite distinctive and can be identified with certainty. Fragments of these wares have been found at Gwithian and Carn Brea, where their shape set the pattern for imitations from local clay. The hilltop enclosure in Dorset, which much later developed into the Iron Age hill fort of Maiden Castle, has produced Neolithic pottery from the Lizard, as has Windmill Hill, the causewayed camp in Wiltshire which gave its name to the first Neolithic

culture to be identified in southern Britain. The Carbon-14 dates for the production of this pottery in the Lizard have been given as about 4000 – 3300 BC.

Fossil pollen analysis, especially of old land surfaces sealed under barrows or similar deposits, has revealed much information about the landscape, and also of the farming of the time. Early corn-growing seems to have taken place, particularly in clearings made in areas of forest and scrub. This showed very well at Gwithian in the Neolithic context. Here, amid so much else, was found a round hut (in a period when most others seem to have been nearer the rectangular) which had been rebuilt and strengthened. It was complete with hearth, and produced a greenstone axe, sherds of beakers and other pottery of the period, bones of domestic animals and fragments of a quern.

The people were probably contemporaries of the men who made the little strip fields at Stannon. The picture that emerges is of an economy of mixed farming, with corn-growing,

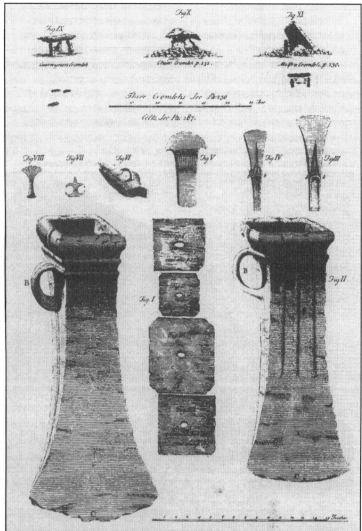

Left: Carn Brea, near Redruth. An upland site among the western, archaeologically richer half of the county, it has yielded Neolithic artefacts, hut circles, and one of the largest hilltop forts with a double rampart and ditch. Part of a medieval castle and a nineteenth-century monument add to the profusion.

Above: Page from *Antiquities, Historical and Monumental, of the County of Cornwall* (1769) by William Borlase. The eighteenth-century antiquary's collection of three 'cromlehs' appear to have been the product of exact observation. He associates them with a sequence of metal axes, progressing from a very early one (Fig V) to various patterns used in the Late Bronze Age. We know that moulds found at Michaelstow produced axes like these later types.

animal husbandry, and woodland management – activities which created a demand for the superior polished stone implements by which the New Stone Age is recognized.

As well as the farmers, it would also appear that there were groups of craftsmen making the polished greenstone axes, and potters in the Lizard making wares from gabbroic clays in sufficient quantity to sustain a long-distance trade. For a time at least, some innovations seem to have spread from Cornwall eastwards, rather than in the opposite direction. These exchange networks suggest large-scale social organization, of a kind compatible with the scale of effort needed to build the Megalithic (Big Stone) tombs.

Great Stone Tombs

Called such names in the past as 'cromlechs' or 'druids' houses', the great prehistoric tombs still hold many mysteries for us today. Cornish barrows are normally round, or at least oval, rather than long like most of the long barrows of Wessex. Classification by structure shows a considerable range of varieties.

'Passage graves' are those where a stone-lined passage leads to a burial chamber. Very similar, but without the chamber, are the 'covered galleries'. Those with a chamber of big stones, but no passage entrance, are called 'closed chambers', and sometimes have a false entrance.

Some of these have an ante-chamber before the chamber proper. Others, with a short passage only, are known as 'entrance graves'. Scilly has an amazing number of them, and these are steadily being excavated.

Because of its wealth of moorstone building blocks, and many fragmented Neolithic communities,

Cornwall has a splendid legacy of these smaller boulder-built or megalithic tombs, exceeded only by the fine collection of tombs on Scilly. Perhaps the best Cornish example to inspect is Trethevy Quoit at St Cleer, east Cornwall. (The local name 'quoit' presumably comes from the shape of the capstone.) The tomb has been

Trethevy Quoit. Just off the edge of the granite moor in St Cleer, east Cornwall, it survives as a particularly good specimen. The rear stone has fallen and the capstone has slipped somewhat as a result. Access from the ante-chamber to the main chamber is through a hole where the corner of the partition slab is missing. The quoit stands in a long oval field, which may once have been a long barrow.

erected from giant slabs of granite or moorstone. These were presumably available nearby, and show some signs of having been shaped with tools. The back slab has fallen in, and the rear of the capstone has consequently slipped down a little, but there is still a very impressive chamber with a smaller ante-chamber. Communication between the two is possible through a hole where the corner of the dividing slab appears to have been removed, either by men or by natural processes. Trethevy Quoit is a 'portal dolmen' type of tomb, so named because two of the slabs supporting the capstone resemble entrance portals. The hole connecting the two chambers at Trethevy may have served the function of a 'porthole' as in some of the French chambered tombs. Perhaps, too, the great holed stone of Men-an-tol in Madron Parish was used in this way. Magical powers were traditionally attached to these stones: passing through the hole in Men-an-tol was deemed to be a sovereign

Men-an-tol, near Land's End, is probably a group of stones from a megalithic tomb. The 'porthole' stone was probably for access to a chamber, but we cannot be sure that the present arrangement is the work of the original builders. Legends survive of magical healing powers, and children were passed through the porthole as a safeguard against rickets.

remedy for rickets or rheumatism!

The most massive of the quoits is at Pawton, above Wadebridge. The capstone (now broken, alas) is two feet thick. The closest in design to Trethevy Quoit is probably Zennor in the far west, near to the village of that name, which has a more complete ante-chamber, though it appears to have been a false entrance. Chun Quoit, near St Just, is similar in construction but has only one closed chamber.

The best-known of the Cornish tombs is Lanyon Quoit near Morvah, and the present monument results from attempts to reconstruct a ruinous tomb in 1824. Quite close to Zennor is Mulfra Quoit with a lofty hilltop setting; as at Zennor, the capstone has slipped.

The megalithic tombs in Scilly are three times as numerous as those of Cornwall. Scilly appears to have been first colonized when megalithic tombs were already familiar sights in Cornwall, and the communities on Scilly seem to have continued to use them in spite of changing fashions on the mainland. It used to be thought that megalithic tombs were designed to serve a whole community, or at least the higher social classes, as collective graves. Alternatively they were thought of as the graves of kings. They are still regarded as aristocratic collective tombs of some kind, but were probably no less important as symbols of territorial ownership.

In the third millennium BC burial customs, and presumably religious beliefs, changed. The new burials, sometimes of a solitary nature, tended to be made under earthen round barrows, and the corpse was often provided with a ritual drinking vessel, a finely made pot or 'beaker'. The individual was placed in a 'cist', a stone box or at least a well-formed grave, under a simple mound. This was considered to be the work of the now-controversial Beaker People, once regarded as new settlers who appeared to have different beliefs

Above: Zennor Quoit, south-west from St Ives, is a big rectangular chambered tomb, set in a large round barrow. It is one of the few to have yielded dating material: pottery of the New Stone Age, and a cremation burial.

Below: Chun Quoit, in Morvah parish. This, like Zennor, is a chambered megalithic tomb clearly set in a round barrow; the barrow is about 35ft (10m) across.

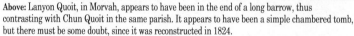

Above: Lanyon Quoit, in Morvah, appears to have been in the end of a long barrow, thus contrasting with Chun Quoit in the same parish. It appears to have been a simple chambered tomb, but there must be some doubt, since it was reconstructed in 1824.

Below: Mulfra Quoit, in Madron parish, appears to have been yet another large, closed chamber tomb in a round barrow some 40ft (12m) across. One side of the capstone now rests on the ground where it has slipped.

Shown here are two famous megalithic monuments – Lanyon, above, and 'Senar' (Zennor) – drawn and recorded by Borlase before 1768 when they were in better condition than they are today. Zennor Quoit, with its smaller ante-chamber, is a fine example of a 'portal dolmen', if Borlase's plan is accurate. His version of Lanyon encourages us to accept the 1824 reconstruction. From *Antiquities*.

which replaced the old customs and emphasized the individual rather than the group in burial rites.

Relatively few Cornish barrows, however, are Beaker burials. As more round barrows have been excavated, the structurally simple domed mound becomes increasingly rare. Most barrows now seem to show long separate phases of construction, with elements like stake rings, which might be added and removed again after intervals, encircling stone rings, and pits and ditches with fires. Also revealed in excavation are secondary cremations or burials, some of them in coffins, and various offerings such as pebbles, beads or scraps of metal.

Much of the tradition of the great tombs as cult centres seems to have survived in Cornwall alongside what Beaker influence there was. The archaeologist Paul Ashbee has suggested that we would do better to think of all earth- and stone-built long barrows as repositories and cult structures rather than as graves. He has also suggested that they may have been built in the hope of restoring fertility to soil destroyed by the first farmers.

What may have been the richest barrow burial in Cornwall, at Rillaton on the eastern edge of Bodmin Moor, produced the famous ribbed and handled gold cup now prominently displayed in the British Museum. It was discovered in 1818 on Duchy land, and rediscovered in this century, between the World Wars, in a royal palace.

The chamber in the barrow has been reconstructed from the memory of a very old man who had witnessed its opening in his youth. Also found in the tomb was a Bronze Age dagger, very characteristic of its time, and some glass beads. These sound like the 'faience' beads of glassy vitrified paste, coloured blue with a tin pigment, which have been found in other barrows of the period. There has been much earnest debate over whether or not such beads were brought to western Britain by traders

Above: The Rillaton Cup, a ribbed and handled gold cup found in Rillaton Barrow at Minions, on the edge of Bodmin Moor. Its rivetted and ribbed construction suggests that it may have come from Mycenae in Greece.

Right: Portrait of Richard Carew, author of the masterpiece *A Survey of Cornwall* (1601). The picture still hangs in the family's present home, Antony House, near Torpoint.

and metal-prospectors from ancient Mycenae. They seem to have been relatively common at one time in Cornwall. When Richard Carew wrote his masterly *Survey of Cornwall* in the sixteenth century they were called 'snakestones', because the most common type was segmented; this was explained in folklore as the product of a snake sloughing its skin around a hazel or other twig. As cures for

snake-bite they were much sought-after:

'Beasts which are stung being given to drink of water wherin this stone hath been soaked, will therethrough recover,' wrote Carew. Some forty years ago a jeweller friend in Bodmin told me that such beads were still found from time to time on the moors around Cardinham, but were usually kept secret and guarded for their magical powers.

Stone Circles and Other Ritual Sites

In the late Neolithic period began the building of big ritual constructions, which seem to have retained and enhanced their importance over many generations. This development started with the 'henges', roughly circular ditches with banks usually outside them. Cornwall has three known examples: Castlewick near Callington, Castilly in Luxulyan, and the Stripple Stones on Hawkstor in the centre of Bodmin Moor, near Temple. The latter contains the remnants of a circle of standing stones, and these may well have been an addition to the earlier bank and ditch, as at Stonehenge. Some authorities regard such henges as the oldest British temples, and as the forerunners of the more familiar stone circles. On the whole, stone circles are later than henges, and they are very numerous in Cornwall. It is also probable that, hidden in the bracken and other moorland overgrowth, many other examples still await discovery.

At some sites, for instance the Merry Maidens in Penwith, a circle is accompanied by one or two other detached stones which may be associated with the monument. There is a legend that maidens were turned to stone for dancing on the Sabbath, and at Penwith the taller detached pair of stones, the Pipers, are two musicians who suffered the same fate for playing for the dance.

There are two standing stones outside the circles at the Hurlers, the group of three stone circles by Minions, near St Cleer; they are said to be two players who ran for it but failed to get away in time. The version of the legend at the Hurlers, as recorded by Carew, was that the people who were turned into stone for Sabbath-breaking were not dancers but men 'hurling', in Cornwall a primitive form of all-in football, very much in spirit like Australian Rules

football, as distinct from the Irish game of the same name which is a type of field hockey. In any event we can be sure that such legends did not appear until long after the true functions of the monument had been forgotten.

The three circles at the Hurlers appear to have been roughly aligned, and seem to point in the general direction of the Rillaton barrow, mentioned above. Part of the ground in the middle circle was paved, and originally there may have been more paving.

Cornish stone circles fall into two main concentrations: one in the far west, where the megalithic tombs are so plentiful, and the other on and around Bodmin Moor. One of the best examples in the former group is the Boscawen-un circle. This has a quartz pillar, now tilting, in its centre which is taller than the stones of the surrounding circle. One of the smallest is at Duloe, at the other end of the county, and consists entirely of lumpy quartz boulders. The use of quartz stones and pebbles in the building and embellishment of ancient monuments was common in

Ireland and Scotland too, and the sparkling whitish stone seems to have had a particular ritual significance.

Unlike Devon and the Lake District, where stone circles are also plentiful, stone alignments are represented in Cornwall only by the Nine Maidens on Goss Moor, near St Columb Major. The same name and number are attached to many stone circles also, but this appears to be because the words are a corruption of the Cornish equivalent of 'standing stones', and, despite some misleading 'restorations', the 'nine' has nothing to do with the number; 'maedn' is late Cornish for 'stone'.

Some stone circles, made up of a very large number of small irregularly shaped stones, such as occur at Fernacre, on the moor between Rough Tor and Garrow, are sometimes thought to be merely the revetment or banking of now-denuded barrows. A few of the single standing stones appear to have been erected as grave markers, and some at the centre of barrows. The evidence for the relation of stone circles to barrows is so varied that little generalization is

Far left, top: The Merry Maidens stone circle, between Penzance and Land's End, is one of the best preserved. The stones are well trimmed and, judged by their even distribution, all survive. The name 'maiden' comes from the Cornish word for 'stone'.

Far left: On the southern edge of the granite mass of Bodmin Moor, near Minions village, stand the Hurlers, three stone circles roughly aligned on the barrow in which the famous Rillaton gold cup was found. An unusual feature is that part of the middle circle appears to have been paved; on the whole, though, the stones are not as well shaped and dressed as many other circles.

Top: Between Penzance and Land's End, the stone circle of Boscawen-un has a central pillar, now tilted, which may or may not be part of the original. The circle is also sometimes known as the Nine Maidens.

Above left: The stone circle at Duloe is one of Cornwall's smallest. It compensates for this by being constructed of quartz stone, the glistening whiteness of which seems to have given it a special ritual value; this stone was used in several barrows.

Above: Blind Fiddler – a standing stone between Land's End and Penzance, so called because of its shape.

yet possible. Some single stones may be ancient boundary markers or linked to ritual uses.

The Age of Bronze

The widespread appearance of Beaker pottery was accompanied by the early use of metal, first copper and then bronze. Rituals changed, and a type of ceremonial weapon was introduced which carried the craft of making stone implements almost to the level of high abstract art. The polished stone battleaxe, often double-bladed, and the stone mace-head, drilled to fit a haft, give clues to their age by the shape of the drill hole. The earliest specimens have waisted holes, produced by a solid drill with sand abrasive. The haft hole was drilled from each side, the two holes meeting in the middle and making a characteristic hour-glass shape. Later, a parallel-sided hole was produced by using a hollow drill with the sand. Most of the surviving specimens are too perfect for them ever to have been put to practical use, and they must have been owned as status symbols. They mark the long transition from the New Stone Age into the Bronze.

The burial of the Copper and Bronze Age dead under earthen barrow mounds, or under heaps of stones or cairns, seems to have begun in Cornwall around 2500 BC and the practice lasted for a millennium and a half at least. Some barrows and cairns are found singly, but more often they are grouped in cemeteries, often situated on hillcrests or headlands. It is amazing how many survive in Cornwall considering that it is not long ago that 'ploughing out a barrow' was a routine farming operation. They were treated as muck-heaps, and their contents were spread on the fields as manure. Only the superstitions that clung to these graves of ancient men can have saved the many that were saved; even so, large numbers of those that remain have been robbed.

Some twenty to thirty barrows were irresponsibly destroyed in Newquay before the Second World War to make a car park for a garage. Some of those that remained were converted into traps for clay-pigeon shooting for the RAF Initial Training Wings. Home Guard machine-gun posts and others for the Observer Corps accounted for more, probably because of their excellent siting. The location of the tombs in prominent positions suggests that they were originally regarded as important territorial symbols, watching over the communal farming territories. Later in the Bronze Age, inhumation was partially replaced by cremation, but round barrows were still used over the urns containing the ashes.

On the land, when it was found how much stronger and more efficient copper became at taking and holding a cutting edge when some ten per cent tin was added, Cornwall should have enjoyed a tin boom on a scale with the Shetlands and their oil today. As yet, however, there is very little archaeological evidence for the extraction and working of tin in Bronze Age Cornwall. Old tin stream works have been turned over again and again by successive generations right up to the present century, often in the belief that tin waste, if left alone, would grow fresh tin from the bottom. In the process, these recent operations took away the evidence of early man's metallurgy that was still very visible in Carew's time:

'They maintain those works to have been very ancient, and first wrought by the Jews with pickaxes of holm, box and hartshorn; they prove this by the names of those places yet enduring ... and by those tools daily found amongst the rubble of such works ... there are also taken up in such works, certain little tools' heads of brass, which some term thunder axes, but they make small show of any profitable use.'

Probably, among all the profusion of hut circles close to every tin-bearing stream, there is evidence enough of Bronze Age tin-working if only there were the resources to make an effective exploration of the sites. The Bronze Age settlers on Rough Tor were pastoralists, but it is hard to believe that they stayed up on one of the only two Cornish mountains – until they were driven away by climatic changes that brought the blanket bog – unless they were there primarily for the tin gravels so close to where their huts were placed. They have left behind a remarkable settlement which shows its details more clearly every year, thanks to the close cropping of the grazing animals.

On the north-west side of Little Rough Tor are a number of what appear to be clearance cairns, heaps of surface moorstone which has been collected and piled to clear the pasture. These cairns have been linked by dry-stone walls, rather like the huts on the far, sunny side of a big reave (large Bronze Age stone boundary wall) that runs down the flank of the hill. This arrangement of the huts means that they were grouped around a small paddock or compound, very like some of the present-day villages in parts of Africa. There is an enormous amount yet to be learned from this very rich site in future excavations.

About 1000 BC peat formation and the creeping blanket bog made the moor virtually uninhabitable. So ended the Middle Bronze Age in east Cornwall.

Bronze tools and weapons dating from about 750 BC, and of patterns and types associated with the Late Bronze Age, have been found in greater numbers than those from the Middle period. An example is the pair of moulds for socketed axes discovered in a quarry near Michaelstow. There are also signs of denser population and more intensive farming during this time, especially in west Cornwall. Settled farming would have been impossible without the ability to enforce some sort of territorial rights, if only to safeguard growing crops. Elaborate and extensive systems of land division have been demonstrated from the study of reaves or boundary banks on Dartmoor and elsewhere in southern Britain. A similar system seems to be emerging in west Cornwall where it may reflect the need to define and safeguard communal territories. It is probably due to these circumstances, with rising population and competition for land resources, that the building and improvement of so many hill forts took place – a theory which grew more powerful as Carbon-14 dating of hill forts began to suggest origins earlier than the Iron Age. On the other hand, despite the conflicts of the first millennium BC, trading contacts with Brittany seem to have flourished right up until Caesar's destruction of the ships of the Breton tribe, the Veneti, in 56 BC.

The Age of Iron

When the employment of iron for useful implements began about 650BC, bronze continued in demand for prestigious and practical purposes. In a society concerned above all with war and women, highly decorated harness mounts, chariot fittings such as linch-pins to hold the wheels on, and shield fittings, survive alongside cosmetic tweezers and superbly designed mirrors. A fine bowl from this school was found at Warbstow in north Cornwall where cliff castles and hill forts are particularly common; the bowl can now be seen in the Royal Institution in Truro. During the first fifty years of the Christian era this school blossomed into what the late Sir Cyril Fox called the last phase of Early Celtic Art.

During the Iron Age, Cornwall appears to have had a varied and mixed range of communities. Some families seem to have lived in isolated huts, or in tiny clusters of them, a constant feature in the Cornish settlement pattern, and at this period people often worked land first cleared in the Bronze Age. Hill-slope enclosures belonging to the Iron Age usually have several rings of

surrounding banks with the huts standing inside. They are not sited according to military considerations but where it suited the farmer, usually at a height between 200ft and 400ft (60m and 120m) above sea level.

Lacking arable fields, but with banks designed to help with herding animals, these hill-slope enclosures seem to have been built at the heart of quite large pastoral farms. Farmsteads built inside a single bank-and-ditch enclosure are known as 'rounds', whatever the shape of the enclosure. Carloggas at St Mawgan-in-Pydar is a well-known example. Among its round huts inside the bank was one used for metal-working.

These 'rounds' could be very long-lived. Castle Gotha near St Austell was occupied in the Bronze Age and lasted into Roman times, and rounds were common in the Romano-British period.

Hill forts began to appear in the second half of the second millennium BC, and in increasing numbers in the course of the Iron Age. In some places they took over sites which had been occupied or even

defended in much earlier periods, as at Carn Brae. In east Cornwall, near Minions, is Stowe's Pound which contains the Cheese Wring, a pile of naturally weathered stones, constructed by building very substantial dry-stone banks to link natural cliff-like defences. It appears to contain hut circles and at least one cairn. It is thought to date from the Bronze Age for it looks out over the Rillaton Barrow and the Hurlers to the great tin dyke, one of the richest tin-bearing gravels on the moor. At the opposite end of the county, between St Ives and Penzance, is another hill fort with stone walls, in a remarkably fine state of preservation and belonging to the National Trust: Trencrom.

Iron Age occupation has been established at many other hilltop forts and hill-slope villages: at Carn Brea itself; Castledore, above Fowey; Tregear Rounds in north Cornwall near St Kew, and also at some cliff castles. In addition, many more open sites, consisting of either isolated farmsteads or small hamlets, were in occupation at the same time, some of them being a continuation from the Bronze Age.

This bronze bowl found at Warbstow, in north Cornwall, is an example of the work of the school of Cornish bronzesmiths who produced highly decorative work for native consumption during the Iron Age. It is now in the Royal Institution, Truro.

The hill forts certainly have the appearance of centres of power. Possibly they served as sub-tribal centres inside the Dumnonian territory that appeared in the centuries before the Roman invasion of Britain.

Cliff castles are very similar to hill forts, and were cheaper to construct because the sea guarded most of the perimeter, fortification only being called for on the land neck that gave access to the headland. The National Trust owns a particularly fine one at Gurnard's Head in Morvah, north of St Just-in-Penwith. The Trust also owns The Rumps, near Polzeath, which was the subject of excavation a few years ago.

It used to be thought that the cliff castles with triple ramparts and ditch were constructed by refugees from Brittany in Caesar's Gallic War. It is now thought that they were chosen as living-sites by pastoralists, and possibly traders who immigrated from Brittany much earlier, and later modified the pastoralist's simple wall to make an enclosure for cattle into a formidable fort by the addition of two substantial ramparts and ditches suitable for the age of sling warfare. The excavation at The Rumps established such a history, and parallels have been established elsewhere. The huts

Above: Gurnard's Head, near Zennor. A headland could be easily converted into a cliff castle by fortifying it at its narrowest point near the shore. The bigger cliff castles, such as Gurnard's Head, Trevelgue and The Rumps, all had places where the occupants could escape by sea in an emergency. The Cornish cliff castles are now thought to have been introduced by immigrants from Brittany.
Above right: The Rumps, near Polzeath. Its ditches and ramparts can be seen on the neck. Beyond them, inside the defended area, archaeologists found the remains of round huts. The inner wall was probably the original one, intended as a cattle fence, then two more ramparts and ditches were added to convert this once-simple enclosure into a fortress.
Right: Treryn Dinas, another of the many ruined fortresses around the Cornish coast.
Far right: Chysauster, off the Penzance – St Ives road. This village was open to the sky with four houses on each side, all facing inwards. The rooms were built within the thickness of the courtyard walls. Villages on this pattern, often with their associated fogou, or secret passage, are unique to the far west of Cornwall where it is likely that more than twenty were inhabited in the late Iron Age and Roman periods.

inside the enclosures showed every sign of peaceful occupation.

At Trevelgue, no less than seven banks were found on the landward side of the cliff castle. The outer two were quite possibly used for enclosing cattle rather than for defence. Inside these, the double and triple banks faced out over formidably deep and steep-sided ditches. These show up dramatically as the sun sinks below the cliffs. Still further inside, a corner of a tiny Roman signal station can be detected, although the greater part of it has gone into the sea. The sea's work goes on, and one of the Iron Age ditches has been deepened by the waves until the headland has become an island.

So far no sign has been found at Cornish hill forts or cliff castles of violent conquest by the Romans, such as has been revealed, for instance, at Maiden Castle in Dorset. When the conquerors of Britain chose to assert their authority over Cornwall, they probably wrecked such native defences as they did not themselves wish to retain, pushing the tops of the ramparts into the ditches and rendering them useless.

Evidence of the Roman conquest in Cornwall shows that it was surprisingly mild. Ordinary life seems to have flowed on without disturbance. The 'courtyard houses'

Fogou at Carn Euny, between Land s End and Penzance. Some of these mysterious underground passages appear to have been designed to trip up intruders with a step hidden in darkness around a corner, but they would have served better as traps than as defences. They occur in a number of Iron Age villages, and other observers have suggested they were used as cold stores or ritual sites.

built in Penwith and Scilly in the Late Iron Age seem to have been inhabited without a break throughout the years of invasion and conquest. Chysauster, probably the best-known village of such houses, reveals an open central courtyard with rooms, built into the thickness of the walls, giving on to it. At Porthmeor a group of courtyard houses was built into a round. Excavation at Carn Euny has shown such houses replacing timber huts from the second century BC and lasting until late in the Roman occupation.

Associated with a number of courtyard houses, although not restricted to the same area and sometimes associated with rounds,

are 'fogous'. These are underground passages constructed by digging a trench, and lining it and roofing it with stone slabs; the walls may be of dry-stone walling, and the whole construction is covered with earth. Brittany has similar but smaller structures which Professor Thomas suggests may be because the continental versions were made by tunnelling rather than by building. Dark, curved, with a step to trip the hurrying intruder, and with mysterious chambers and passages opening on to them, fogous have provoked ingenious theories as to their uses or possible defensive purposes. A favourite modern explanation regards them as ventilated cool-storage areas.

But the archaeologist Mrs P. M. Christie, after excavating the fogou at Carn Euny which has a side passage opening into a chamber, thinks they may have had some ritual usage.

On the eve of the Roman occupation, Cornwall, possibly in harness with Devon as the tribal territory of Dumnonia, had developed its own cultural and social patterns. Links with Ireland, and much more with Brittany, were important, but the Cornish folk, especially those of Penwith in the far west, could already claim to be very different. After the Romans went the Cornish stayed, and stayed different, making a virtue of it, closely guarding their individuality for many centuries to come.

ROMANS AND EARLY CHRISTIANS

The Roman Conquest of Britain had very little effect on Cornwall. Any change that the Romans made passed away quickly when the legions sailed from British shores, and their rule made little difference to the Cornish landscape. It never seemed worthwhile to the Romans, apparently, to master the difficulties of transport along the length of the peninsula by the north-east to south-west routes. This made it more possible for the native population to maintain their overseas connections – via the easier transpeninsular routes running from north-west to south-east – with Ireland and Wales, and south to the Mediterranean. Connections with Brittany were dramatically affected, however, when Caesar destroyed the fleet of the Veneti in 56BC; this action ended the close relationship which had established settlers from Brittany in Cornish cliff castles.

The discovery of the Roman villa at Magor, near Camborne, the only one to be found in the county so far, emphasized how cut-off Cornwall was from the mainstream of life under the Empire. The villa was undoubtedly an imitation of Roman fashion, but was constructed by builders unfamiliar with the normal methods for such buildings. The result was almost more native than Roman. Its design was odd, its layout incompetent, and it was mean in construction. It had a tesselated floor, but a plain one. And even after one main wall collapsed, the archaeological evidence suggests that the ruins were still occupied for some years.

Such evidence as there is of Imperial life in the peninsula is tantalizingly scrappy. West of Bodmin, at Nanstallon, a Roman first-century fort abandoned soon after AD75 had barrack accommodation for some five hundred men, cavalry and infantry. Hearths within the camp suggest some interest in working the tin in the valley gravels nearby. This short-lived attempt to develop Cornwall probably came to an end because of trouble for the government elsewhere.

Ironically, it would appear that the resumption of Roman effort in Cornwall also came about because of disturbances in another part of the Empire. In the third century AD, when inflationary financing was staving off complete economic collapse, the tin that was necessary to debase the silver coinage was lost when barbarians overran the Spanish tin mines. An ingot found at Camanton, near Newquay, bears a stamp which shows that it was Imperial property, and this seems to indicate that Cornwall was then reckoned Imperial territory and not a military frontier zone.

This ingot may be related to the existence of a Roman road in north Cornwall. The name Stratton suggests such a road, and various attempts have been made to trace straight sections of road south-west from that village. Of the five Roman milestones found in Cornwall, two were discovered in the vicinity of Tintagel. There may also have been a ferry across the Camel estuary, as indicated by finds of Roman-British artefacts at Daymer Bay and on the opposite side of the estuary, on a beach near Padstow.

West Cornwall seems to have been involved in this second phase of Roman penetration. Milestones of the third century at Breage, and of the very early fourth century at Hilary, indicate a road running from the St Michael's Mount area to somewhere near Porthleven. Nearby, at Bosence, St Erth, a shaft was discovered containing what appear to be votive gifts of pewter and tin.

Curiously, although the evidence of official Roman interest in Cornish tin is so slight as to suggest that their efforts were tentative and

Above: Celtic cross, near Boscastle Church. Of the numerous crosses still standing in Cornwall, many were erected in the course of missionary ventures into Cornwall in the Dark Ages, others date from the Middle Ages, and the same form was taken up again in this century for war memorials. Some are said to have been preaching crosses, used before churches were built; others may have been markers for ill-defined trackways, or boundary definitions. The example shown here is thought to be early, and has a simple raised cross on a swollen head. **Right and far right:** Celtic crosses at Crows-an-Wra and near the Merry Maidens stone circle.

unsuccessful, there is more evidence in this period of metal-working in native huts, if only on a scale comparable with a village blacksmith in later times. A tin bowl from Treloy, St Columb Minor, other vessels of pewter or tin and moulds for making them confirm that most of the tin-mining in the Roman period was for native use.

The Dark Ages

If Roman Cornwall is difficult to reconstruct from such fragments as are left, Cornwall in the Dark Ages, in some ways the most attractive and fascinating period of her history, is even more inscrutable. The paucity of concrete evidence has served only to

provoke imagination and fantasy to cloud the picture further. Even pottery helps little. Coarse sherds of locally made ware have been found all over Britain on late Roman sites, and are virtually undatable. At Gwithian and other sites with a late Roman element it has been demonstrated that fine imitations of late Roman ware were still being used and made well

probably spasmodically, until AD600 or 700. Here, of course, the Christian influence is important.

There is little indication that Christianity had become established in Cornwall before the withdrawal of the legions from Britain, but the trading contacts of Cornwall in the post-Roman period were with areas, particularly Ireland and the Mediterranean, where the faith had been dominant. Missionaries from Wales and Ireland seem to have been at work in Cornwall as early as the fifth century. They have left traces of their passage not only in dedications of churches but also in documents recording the lives of the saints, where place-names may enable at least some history to be distilled from romantic fantasy.

The Celtic Church that survived in Ireland, despite the efforts of St Patrick, a foreigner from Britain, decided to organize itself in a manner very different from the Roman Catholic Church of the Late Roman Empire. Whereas the latter was organized on the territorial basis of the diocese, which it adopted from the Imperial system of government, the Celtic Church was tribal and monastic. The church and monastery were often regarded as the property of the family which had originally endowed them. The Celtic bishop was a member of the monastery, subordinate to the abbot except when he performed special functions in services which required a bishop.

The saints of the Celtic Church seem to have been anyone who was committed to a religious life. All were expected to take up a pilgrimage, when they would leave their own monastery, go off among the heathen to preach, convert, teach, found a new church and monastery, and then go off again and repeat the process.

A special feature of their way of life was fierce asceticism. When St Petroc first met St Sampson he found him in an icy hill stream where he stood up to his neck daily

after the fourth century. In a period when good pottery was scarce, to judge from the sherds that remain, we have little idea how long a fourth-century pot might have remained in use. Similarly, finds of grass-marked ware, which has tell-tale marks on its base where the freshly thrown pot rested on a bed of chopped grass while drying, have been dated to about AD600. However, Professor Thomas has shown that some of it was still being produced and used in the late seventh and early eighth centuries.

The grass-marked pottery suggests that contacts with Ireland were being maintained. Fragments of imported ware, both fine and coarse, indicate that trade in luxuries from the Mediterranean continued,

between three in the morning and cock-crow, to mortify the flesh. The account of St Sampson's work among the heathen of north Cornwall illustrates a method that they shared with missionaries from Rome. Up on the moor he came upon a party dancing round a standing stone, which to him was obviously a horrid idol. After stopping the obscene dancing, he Christianized the site and took it over for God by carving a cross on the back of the stone. This was the policy urged on Augustine by Gregory the Great, to establish churches where the people had been accustomed to come for their old heathen worship, and so take over the goodwill belonging to the site. Augustine himself seems to have carried this out when he founded his first monastery to St Peter and St Paul at Canterbury. For, buried under his first church on the site, a broken standing stone was found.

In the sub-Roman period the old routes of the Bronze Age re-emerged to bring both immigrants and the new faith to Cornwall. The obvious points of entry from Ireland, the Camel and Hayle estuaries, became the reception areas. To the former came Brocagnus, otherwise Brychan of Wales, where he is said to have been a king, and with him he brought a round dozen of daughters and another of sons, all of whom became saints, and many of whom left dedications in walking distance of Padstow Harbour: St Endellion, St Minver, St Teath, St Mabyn, St Kew, St Issey, and, perhaps within two days' walking, St Ive. Unique dedications seem to indicate an early foundation. Where multiple dedications occur along the main routes, these do not necessarily testify to missionary journeys. After all, St Petroc is said to have remained at Padstow for thirty years, and he can hardly have spent similar periods at his other churches.

One type of evidence in the west and south-west suggests that Irish influence waxed as Roman waned. Memorial stones with inscriptions in Ogham, an alphabet made up of straight lines, long and short, at right angles or sloping, incised along a line or at the edge of the stone, sometimes have Irish names in the inscription. Sometimes the inscription is repeated or paraphrased in Latin capitals, sometimes in a more flowing script called Hiberno-Saxon. More than three hundred such stones have been recorded in Ireland, less than fifty in England and Wales, and half a dozen in Cornwall.

A particularly good example is to be found at St Endellion, near the churchyard at the cross-roads on the way to Port Quin. As its crosshead it has an open Chi-Rho monogram. The Chi-Rho is an early Christian symbol made up from the first two letters of Christ's name in Greek. Running vertically down the face, in letters that show the early influence of Hiberno-Saxon, is the

This plate from William Borlase's *Antiquities of Cornwall* (1769) assembles drawings of half a dozen inscribed stones from the early post-imperial years. The lettering has been somewhat tidied up, and is easier to read on the drawing than on the stones themselves. The second from the left is the so-called Tristan Stone from Menabilly East Lodge Gate, near Fowey. The inscription in Borlase's day was read as: 'CIRUSIUS HICIACIT CUNOWORI FILIUS'. But the 'W' in the name is an inverted 'M'; if the beginning is also reversed, this makes an initial 'D', and on the stone itself the rest of the first name is sufficiently unclear to be read as 'Drustaus' or 'Drustans', i.e. an early form of Tristan.

inscription: 'BROCAGNUS HIC IACIT NADOTTIFILIUS' (Here lies Brocagnus son of Nadottus). On the corner of the stone the same inscription appears in Ogham.

There are many more inscribed memorial stones of the sixth century which have no 'oghams'. A few, thought to be very early, have clear Roman capital letters, but most appear to have been cut by illiterate masons from indifferent copy. Some have very Roman-sounding names like Licinius the Legate, whose stone is almost hidden along the river bank near Slaughter Bridge, not far from Camelford.

The earliest, thought to date from around AD500, have characteristically good-quality Roman lettering, horizontal wording, and a relatively elaborate text. Perhaps, on these grounds, the oldest is at Carnsew, near Hayle. It reads: 'CUNAIDE HIC IN TUMULO IACIT VIXIT ANNOS XXXIII' (Cunaide lies here in the tomb; (s)he

lived for thirty-three years). Texts such as this one use formulae employed by Christians elsewhere; others use forms reminiscent of the pagans; many use both.

Some of the later inscriptions seem to hint at the emergence of native kings, e.g. 'Rialobran son of Cunovalus'. This name is thought to mean 'Royal Raven'. It is a very famous stone and the down in Penwith where it stands is called after it 'Men Scryfa' (the stone with writing).

The memorial stone which has received most attention in the last fifty years is the so-called Tristan Stone. It now stands at Menabilly East Lodge Gate near Fowey but it was originally further along the ridgeway at Castledore. On the back is a Greek Tau cross, a very old Christian symbol, quite compatible with an early sixth-century date and missionary influence. Weathering of the moorstone has made the inscription very difficult to decipher,

though this can never have been an easy task since the mason who cut the letters appears to have been a confused illiterate. He has, for instance, inverted a letter 'M', making a 'W' which the alphabet did not then have.

Attempts to read the first name on the stone at one time made it Cirusius, or something similar. When Castledore was scientifically excavated no effort was spared to get a better reading and photograph. This produced Drustaus or Drustans, which is most acceptable as an early sixth-century form of Tristan. He is recorded in the rest of the inscription as 'son of Cunomorus'. In the life of St Pol de Leon (St Paul Aurelian) we hear how the saint visited Marcus Cunomorus at Lancien. This name still survives as Lantyne, which was in historical times a principal manor nearby. From this it has been argued that King Mark of Cornwall and his son Tristan are the persons mentioned on the stone, that Mark ruled his

Some of this collection of inscribed stones from Borlase's book date from the end of the Dark Ages. The second from the left reads 'DONIERT ROGAVIT PRO ANIMA' and is said to refer to King Dumgarth of Cornwall, who was drowned late in the ninth century AD.

territories from Castledore, the large rectangular building discovered there being his palace, and that the Giant's Hedge, which runs from the Fowey peninsula to Looe, was a boundary of his territories.

This modern reading, if it is correct, makes a new difficulty for us by calling Tristan Mark's son, for the legend and romances firmly describe him as a nephew. This has been argued away as the softening of a reality too scandalous to be contemplated at a time when the missionary Celtic Church was trying to fix moral standards. The idea of Tristan running off with his new and beautiful step-mother (Iseult) could not be tolerated.

Whatever the historical reality behind the stories of Mark, Tristan and Iseult, their setting in Cornwall seems secure. The *Life of St PaulAurelian* tells us further of Mark worshipping at St Sampson's Church, to which Iseult gave her best dress to be displayed there at festivals. In nearby Golant the church is dedicated to Sampson. West of the Fowey peninsula, near Truro, is Moresk Wood, called Morais in Domesday, which to all appearances is the Forest of Morrois where the lovers fled and were discovered by Mark. The river crossing at La Mal Pas corresponds to the modern Malpas; the White Land appears to be a translation of the modern place-name, Chirgwin in Cornish. Carhurles, which some think

was the older name for Castledore, has been credited with deriving from Gorlois, who married King Arthur's mother. The link this would make with the place-names connected with Mark, is reinforced by the name Kilmarth, the 'Home of Arthur', not far from Castledore. Kelliwic Rounds in north Cornwall, traditionally an Arthurian stronghold, would also make sense, bearing much the same relation to the route across the peninsula at its northern end as Castledore does in the south.

If the stories of Tristan and Iseult have no truth behind them, their author seems to have woven them into a real place, and based most of the action in an area where a local ruler commanded the southern end of one of the main trans-peninsular routes to Ireland, the home of the heroine. The Arthurian romances, on the other hand, have spawned place-names of an entirely different order of fantasy. King Arthur's Bed is nothing like a bed, but an oversized, man-shaped hole worn into a slab of moorstone in the remote past by dripping water (it is located on the eastern side of Bodmin Moor near Trewortha). King Arthur's Hall, a mysterious prehistoric stone-lined enclosure, is certainly no hall, and was already ancient in the traditional time of Arthur's exploits. Arthur's Grave, in north Cornwall, appears to be a megalithic tomb with a hilltop fort constructed round it. Such names

may help the tourist industry, but they add to the mist which obscures any possible historic Arthur. Only the connections which have a Cornish derivation make any sense in linking Arthur with Cornwall.

The first mention of Arthur in a literary source is in Nennius's *History of the Britons,* a ninth-century edition of a late seventh-century collection of historical material. Here Arthur appears as a sub-Roman cavalry leader, born into a Cornish Royal line. He led the British kings for a time in successful resistance to the barbarian Anglo-Saxons. Archaeology suggests that the advancing Saxons were indeed turned back, some even returning to the Frisian Islands off the Dutch coast during the first half of the sixth century. On that basis there *could* be an historical figure whose doings gave rise to the legends of Arthur.

In 1113 the suggestion by visiting canons from Laon that Arthur was no longer alive provoked a riot in Cornwall. The legend must have had deep roots there before the addition of the wilder embellishments. These were developed in their most extravagant form by Geoffrey of Monmouth to satisfy the needs of Henry II for propaganda at once nationalistic and also glorifying Henry's Angevin dynasty.

More impossible deeds were credited to Arthur than were scored by almost all previous heroes of romance, both real and imaginary. The result has been to turn Arthur into something quite unbelievable. But it is hard not to believe that there was someone there in the shadows of the Dark Ages. The problem is to get to him through other, more plausible sources.

ARTHURES HALL.

King Arthur's Hall, a mysterious monument on a saddle on the moor above St Breward. A rectangle about 60ft by 35ft (18m by 10m) has been enclosed by slabs of moorstone set on edge. Much of the interior space is occupied by water. No-one knows who made the 'Hall', nor when nor why. The illustration is from an engraving by the cartographer John Norden (1548–1626).

FARMING THE MOORS

When Rome fell, barbarian kingdoms emerged in the west, and Cornwall, along with Devon and probably part of Somerset, emerged as the Kingdom of Dumnonia, on lines very similar to the pre-Roman tribal territory. Dumnonia east of the Tamar was the obvious territory for Wessex to expand into, and when Ine was King of Wessex we hear of Geraint of Dumnonia holding the line of the Tamar against him. Dumnonia then became more purely Cornish.

According to Welsh annals, Dumgarth, King of Cornwall, was drowned in action about 871. He has been identified as the king 'Doniert' whose memorial stone of granite, decorated with interlace and inscribed in Latin 'Doniert ordered me for [the good of his] soul', stands in a space cleared from the hedgerow in St Cleer parish on the road to Redgate.

The Cornish proved very difficult to hold down. Overrun by Egbert, King of Wessex, in 814, they were put down with great slaughter in a rebellion of 825, probably near Camelford, perhaps at Slaughter Bridge, a mile up the Camel from the town. It was not until 838 that Egbert finally broke their power at Hingston Down in south-east Cornwall, after the Cornish had taken the opportunity brought by Danish raiders to revolt again. Probably the event that did most to unite Cornwall with Saxon Wessex was when Athelstan, grandson of King Alfred, set up a new see at St Germans with a Cornish bishop, Conan.

Professor Thomas has detected a pattern of repetition and continuity in Cornish social development that lasted from the Bronze Age until well into the Middle Ages. Partly this was the result of the local geology and topography: the same coastal plains with good soil were there in any age, the same hillsides for pastoral farming, and all

The mountain is Rough Tor. Its lower slopes, to the west and south, are covered with hut circles like that in the foreground of the picture, and in such profusion as to suggest a small town. Further down the slope the gravels along the stream-bed once bore tin.

the time the difficult communications with England.

When England was beaten into new forms of social and political organization by Viking raiders from across the North Sea, Cornwall in its remoteness was very little troubled. The monastery of St Petroc at Padstow was moved to Bodmin after seaborne plunderers had sacked it in AD981. A Viking fleet a few years later raided the coasts, coming down from the north and going round Land's End to the south, but compared with other coastal counties we hear of very little devastation. A hoard of fine church silver from Trewhiddle near St Austell appears to have been deliberately concealed in a moment of danger and not recovered by its owners. But in general Cornish society seems to have come through relatively unscathed.

In the immediate post-Roman period old units of settlement and government, seen previously in the pre-Roman Iron Age, seem to have reasserted themselves or survived and grown stronger again. It is possible that some of these units go back even to the Late Bronze Age. Hill forts were reoccupied. Professor Thomas has shown how within the Kingdom of Dumnonia political divisions on the one hand look back to the earlier tribal divisions, and on the other foreshadow the Saxon division of Cornwall into six Hundreds.

On a domestic level, some of the courtyard houses of Penwith continued in occupation (Porthmeor, for example) until the sixth century. Hill-slope enclosures such as Carloggas, in St Mawgan-in-Pydar, seem to have remained inhabited until about AD 150 at least. However, the enclosed homesteads known as rounds, mentioned earlier, tended to be abandoned and then reoccupied at various times into the Dark Ages, probably because they were built on higher ground and lacked arable field systems. The general drift seems to have been down to the valleys, to farms with field systems that reveal a greater interest in arable farming. In Cornish place-names the syllables 'tre', 'trev' and 'tref' indicate this more open kind of farmstead, and 'car', 'caer' or 'gear' indicate rounds.

Something of the changing patterns of settlement was shown by Professor Thomas after a study of the place-names that featured in the Cornish migration to Brittany in the sixth century. The 'car' or 'caer' names were still dominant at that time, but by the time of the Cornish Domesday Book 31 per cent of the place names mentioned were of the 'tre' or 'trev' type, and only eight of the 'car' type survived.

There was an open settlement at Gwithian, of round houses with stone foundations and turf walls, which continued until the eleventh century. The associated

About three miles south of St Ives, the site of Trencrom hill fort is very easy to reach. The fort was defended by a dry stone rampart linking stretches of natural granite cliff in a single protective wall.

fields suggest that the migration downhill from the rounds was accompanied not only by more arable farming but also by improved techniques of cultivation. Small, square, prehistoric fields were replaced by longer rectangular ones. From the sixth to the ninth centuries the fields of Gwithian were already tilled by a plough which turned furrows. Thereafter narrow ridge-and-furrow appeared, which hitherto had been regarded as characteristic of medieval and early modern fields. The discoveries at Gwithian point to these developments happening much earlier.

The Land of Hamlets

As the various settlements and fields took shape over the centuries, so the foundations were laid of the Cornish landscape as we know it today – the landscape that the historian F. W. Maitland long ago called the 'land of hamlets'. The common unit of settlement in the medieval Cornish countryside seems to have been a hamlet of from two to five houses with their outbuildings. The single isolated farmstead was very rare. Larger settlements were to be found in the most favoured sites, but there were relatively few of them. Many of the smaller sites have increased through the centuries, and larger ones may have shrunk or vanished, but despite the devastating onslaughts of the Plague in the fourteenth century, the hamlet pattern was remarkably persistent.

This may have been because of the limitations on upland sites imposed by soil and climate. Nucleated village sites would have meant too much travelling to and from more distant fields on difficult roads in all conditions – and the weather there can be intimidating. The holding at Irish in St Breward, on the edge of Bodmin Moor, was divided into five in the nineteenth century, but soon amalgamated back to one. The ruins of the other houses can all be traced in the hedgerows, except where one has been converted into a shed. The ancient pattern of settlement re-established itself as if history had moved backwards.

Where nucleated settlements in common fields did provide an alien element in the Cornish landscape was in the towns. Towns were notoriously foreign to Cornwall. Speculating landlords who tried to plant towns in Cornwall had to entice inhabitants for them from across the county boundaries, over the English Channel as well as the Tamar. Breton and English names long remained dominant in the lists of taxpayers for the towns.

Open or common field systems were on the verge of extinction early in the Tudor period. Richard Carew's *Survey of Cornwall,*

The people who lived in the hut circles inside the fort may well have been the creators of the small fields in the middle distance.

published in 1601 although written earlier, corroborates this. Writing of the Cornish husbandmen (i.e. smallholders) he said: 'These in times not past the remembrance of some yet living, rubbed forth their estate in the poorest plight; their grounds lay all in common, or only divided by stitch-meal.' This means land intermingled in strips, as in open or common field systems. Land lying in quillets, a local name for strips, appears surprisingly often, especially in the western manors, in the accurate and beautifully drawn Lanhydrock Atlas which dates from the seventeenth century. The Atlas shows the Robartes estates, and is still kept in their old house, Lanhydrock near Bodmin, now owned by the National Trust and worth the trip for the maps alone.

Some field systems in Cornwall were more short-lived. In one of the most unsuitable places for arable cultivation in the whole county, the centre of Bodmin Moor, the little church and village of Temple nestle in the lee of old fields which stretch up exposed to the south-westerly prevailing gales.

The Crusades had made the Knights Templars popular, and among the gifts of property made to them was this land in a place remote and different from anything else they knew. To anyone up on Hawkstor, across the saddle where the turnpiked A30 runs, in good evening light when conditions of growth are right for the bracken, the whole medieval field system of Temple can show up clearly, except perhaps where there has been very recent ploughing to 'improve' parts of the pasture.

At Temple the site was so impossible that it was probably not cultivated on a common field system

Temple, on Bodmin Moor, from the air. The layout of the medieval arable Fields is reminiscent of the open-field system used in the Midlands. The Knights Templars, given this land in return for their deeds in the Crusades, appear to have developed it on lines familiar to them but foreign to the moor.

after the famines of the early fourteenth century. At most periods when we can glimpse its population it seems to have been almost deserted. Sometimes only a goatherd or two lived there. When William Marshall was making his Survey in 1796 for the Board of Agriculture, he noted the large herds of goats and commented: 'Temple is a deserted village. The only one I have ever seen. Some years ago not a single person lived in the township (a curacy dependent to Blisland) and only one little farmhouse is now inhabited; the ruins of half a dozen more; the body of the church down; the chancel remains; Goldsmith must surely have travelled this road.' (The poet Oliver Goldsmith was currently noted for his poem, 'The Deserted Village', written in 1770.)

The Victorian church lies below the present village in a moorland cleft, and Merrifield, the principal farm, even deeper in its shelter. The lower stages of the church tower seem older, but nothing can now be detected for certain as remaining from the Templars' church. When Carew was writing of it in the sixteenth century, in its decayed state, it seems to have been used as a Gretna Green of the South-West, since it had retained its exemption from the bishop's jurisdiction from Templar days: 'For if common report communicate with truth, many a bad marriage bargain is there yearly slubbered up.' Planted by a distant community, with fields laid out in a fashion learnt in a better climate, it was abandoned to serve as the archetypal deserted medieval village, and as the haunt of shady characters when communications were worse than today.

Much of Bodmin Moor is covered by narrow ridge-and-furrow, in what appear in aerial photographs

Inventory of the 'goods and chatells' of Ralph Sturtridge of the parish of Temple, made in 1685. The document reveals a holding almost entirely dependent on animal husbandry except for a small amount of 'barley and noats'. There is little information about the house, but mention of a feather bed, brass and pewter suggests that at least some of the domestic comforts, noted elsewhere by writers such as Carew, had begun to penetrate as far as Temple.

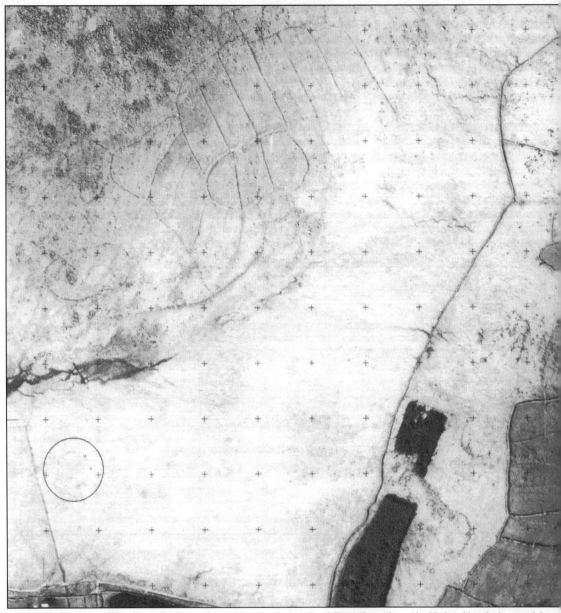

The National Trust has one of the richest sites for the amateur field archaeologist at Rough Tor on the northern side of Bodmin Moor. In the upper left-hand quarter of the aerial photograph are the lower slopes of Rough Tor, densely occupied by hut circles beyond which paddocks, possibly from the Bronze Age, appear to have been re-colonized by several Iron Age homesteads. Most of this partially cleared area was further cleared for the plough in

to be medieval field systems. To the unaided eye on the ground they may be almost invisible, but in the more mountainous parte of the moor the view from the tors, such as Rough Tor or Brown Willy, serves almost as an aerial view. Between these two, on the south-eastern lower slopes of Rough Tor, and on the western lower slopes of Brown Willy, is a series of apparently

medieval field systems, which would have belonged to pioneer farms cut out of the waste. The ruined farmhouses and buildings that remain appear to be much later, from the modern period, when the failed arable land had long been down to grass. The hillside is like a palimpsest, a document where writings from different periods have been set down

on top of each other. Between them these farms span an enormous period of history.

On Rough Tor a series of paddocks, probably from the Bronze Age, has been created by clearing the larger boulders to form oval walls. When, in the High Middle Ages, there were too many mouths to feed and the pioneer farmer set about breaking in

the Middle Ages, producing the narrow curving ridge-and-furrow that shows up so clearly. In the vally between Rough Tor and Brown Willy, the two highest Cornish mountains, is Fernacre stone circle (ringed at bottom left).

the moor, he found that in fields such as this half the work of clearance had been done. The lesser boulders that had been left by the previous wall-builders, could now be cleared to form furlong boundaries without moving them very far at all. Where there was a protuberance from the bed-rock, or from any boulder too large to move, the plough appears to have been brought up as far as possible and then carried over. The ridges are very narrow here, the furrows shallow. Some show the characteristic signature of the medieval plough, a slight curve like a reversed S. The largest paddock on Rough Tor was divided horizontally, and where the plough turned, in the middle and at the lower edge, soil movement has produced a substantial headland. Many furlongs are grouped in threes, suggesting that their unknown medieval cultivator was familiar with the Midland open three-field system. Was he a tinner who came from up-country and had a licence to cultivate moorland waste? There were such. The groups of fields, as well as the scattered farmhouses, suggest single-family farms. With so much waste to choose from, common fields would have had no purpose.

Further down the slope towards the stream, hiding behind two shelter-belts of evergreen conifers, the farm of Fernacre still works. Both the field shapes and some ridge-and-furrow identify it as medieval. The 'acre' element in the name can have the specialist meaning of ploughland. Here the pioneer had cleared his arable from land infested with bracken. W.G. V. Balchin, in *The Cornish Landscape*, describes Fernacre, which was first mentioned in the Subsidy List of 1327, as 'the very frontier of settlement'.

Across the stream from Fernacre, on the lower slopes of Brown Willy, Cornwall's highest mountain, and facing into the prevailing wind, is a string of four deserted farmsteads sitting in their medieval fields. The northernmost is in the middle of its former ploughland. Above, an extensive area of rough moorland grazing, stretching high up the mountainside, is walled in. In the lower part of this, just above the better fields with their clear ridge-and-furrow, is a group of small fields walled off from the rougher grazing (the outfield), and from the lower improved arable (the infield). The field layout suggests an infield/outfield system on the scale of a single family farm. In this type of cultivation the infield was tilled every year, supplemented by intakes from the rough outfield, which were cropped for a few years and then returned as grazing. This system was the alternative kind of open field, favoured for poorer soils, and perhaps also the ancestor of the two- and three-field systems.

The incidence of Black Death – which arrived in England in 1348 and caused repeated epidemics until the seventeenth century – seems to have been very severe in Cornwall, although it appears not to have been the cause of the general economic collapse that occurred elsewhere.

Although Duchy lands in the far west, heavily involved in the production of tin, failed to maintain their previous prosperity, in east Cornwall, where the economy was more diversified with, for instance, shipping, fishing, shipbuilding and textiles, rents were maintained, and vacant land was taken up quite quickly. However, the Black Death marked the end of licences to cultivate the moor. The removal of population pressure halted the advance of the plough into marginal lands.

Retreat from the Moors

After the Black Death, the archaeological evidence in fact suggests a massive retreat from moorland cultivation. This may have been due not only to the catastrophic fall in population, but also to the deterioration of the climate. If the rains that produced the appalling famines of 1315–17 over most of Europe fell proportionately on the moors, they must have rendered them virtually uninhabitable for most of the year. The medieval man on the moor may then have repeated the downhill journey of his Bronze Age ancestor, who left before the creeping advance of the blanket bog.

Summer grazing, established in places such as Twelve Men's Moor by the twelfth and thirteenth centuries, had become more extensive by the time that Carew wrote in his *Survey*: 'The Devonshire and Somersetshire graziers feed yearly great droves of cattle in the North quarter of Cornwall, and utter them at home.' And again; 'The middle part of the shire (saving the enclosures about some few towns and villages) lieth waste and open, sheweth a blackish colour, beareth heath and spiry grass, and serveth in a manner only to summer cattle.'

In his *Diary* for 1576 William Carnsew of Bokelly records on 27 April: 'Cattle to Brown Willy. Sent my cattle to the moor.' In late August he was busy for some days in sorting his sheep out from another grazier's flock on the moor. His own rights extended over an enormous and very wild area, the moors of Hamatethy in St Breward, Rough Tor and Brown Willy. These would be at least six miles from his house at Bokelly, by a very hilly road.

As long as grazing was kept mainly to the summer, the moors remained rough, with heathers, furze and other deep-rooting plants. But by Carew's time, if not before, over-grazing had begun. This was to become worse when farmers started over-wintering their sheep and cattle on the moors as a regular practice. In 1811 Lord de Dunstanville published a new edition of Carew's *Survey*, with notes written by Thomas Tonkin in 1739. From these we can glimpse something of the price paid for the over-grazing of the two previous centuries.

Tonkin displays some confusion in the contemporary accounts of sheep diseases, writing of rot, liver-fluke and even tapeworm when the real trouble was moorland or pining sickness. The latter is due to deficiency of trace elements, specifically cobalt, and this arises from changes in soil and vegetation produced by over-grazing. A hard iron-pan develops below the topsoil, and with the high rainfall the trace elements leach down below. While deep-rooting plants are growing plentifully they bring up sufficient trace elements for the flocks. When the deep-rooting plants go, the sheep develop severe symptoms of pining sickness after less than two months on the moor. A dose of cobalt chloride can produce apparently magical results in a few hours in beasts that were seemingly at death's door. However, the practical methods for coping with this problem were only worked out on Rough Tor Farm by Major Patten after the Second World War. Former generations had found the moor a progressively hostile place for their livestock.

MINING FOR TIN AND COPPER

Seismic forces distributed the mineral lodes in Cornwall, and at the end of the last Ice Age atmospheric forces began to help in the preparation of the ores for the tinner. Cornwall escaped glaciation, but the peri-glacial conditions (on the fringe beyond the permanent ice-sheet) were probably more useful in making tin ore more accessible. The repeated freezing and thawing broke up the lodes as well as the granite moorstone, reducing it to gravel. The heavy run-off from the melting glaciers swept down, and carried the gravels, including the tin ores, to the beds of the swollen rivers and to the valley bottoms. Here the denser tin-stone was precipitated out before the miscellaneous rubbish carried along by the flood.

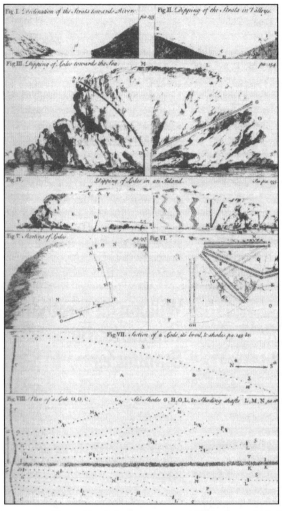

The medieval tinner recognized the work of water in the distribution of the ores. When he went prospecting, he looked over likely hillsides for 'shoad' or waterworn tin-stone which, if followed with the utmost care, might lead him either to the uphill point where the lode lay

Above: In this engraving from his Natural History of Cornwall (1757), Borlase attempts to show the general disposition of many of the lodes (ore deposits) and how these outcrops might be discovered from the distribution of the shoad, or waterworn tin-stone.

hidden, from which the tin-stone had been broken, or it might fan out downhill to gravel in a stream bed. The form extraction would take – tin-streaming or lode-mining – depended on how he made his find.

The process of tin-streaming involved the separation of the tin-ore from the rubbish by hydraulic means. A stream of water can carry more material in suspension the faster it flows. When checked in speed, a stream will tend to

precipitate the densest particles first. So, when the shoad led tinners to a gravel bed they would clear aside the upper layers which contained no ore, and then if possible try to separate the lower gravels by diverting a swift-flowing stream over them. Failing that, they could dam up a reservoir and, when it was full, break the dam so that a fast surge of water would sweep away the lighter particles, leaving a much purer tin. Abandoned earthworks from this method can be seen in all the old areas of tin-streaming.

An alternative method was to dig a pit at the lowest possible point, and divert a stream over the gravels and across the top of the pit. The pit would gradually fill up with tin ore, ready concentrated for the tinner to dig out with his shovel. Larger lumps of ore were broken, in medieval tin-streams, by pounding in mortars of granite; they were then returned to the rest of the gravel that was being processed.

Further separation was accomplished by highly skilled use of the same principle of suspending and progressively precipitating solid particles in water. Cradles and 'buddles', in which the tin was stirred and moved continuously in flowing water, took away the lighter detritus. Most of the tin that escaped in this process was caught by leading the used water down steps of carefully chosen fibrous turves. For further purification there was the tinner's shovel (the vanning shovel), his pan and horsehair sieve. These all used the same principle only on a smaller scale, and achieved a very exact standard of separation.

Under this sort of treatment the Cornish gravels provided a very high-quality ore, from which the worst impurities had been weathered out. At this stage it was known as 'black tin'. When it was smelted into the regulation 3½ hundredweight (178kg) blocks it became 'white tin'. The very best black tin was sent to the blowing-house to produce 'grain tin', used for the highest-quality work, for example for staining glass and manufacturing dyes.

The blowing-houses were small, crudely constructed stone buildings with thatched roofs. A simple furnace of granite burned charcoal, and bellows enabled the exact high temperature to be reached and held. After about seven years' use, it paid the owner to burn down his thatch to recover the particles of tin carried

up there by the draught. After a few years the value of the tin particles would far outweigh the cost of a rough thatched roof.

Of all the factors that made Cornwall different, tin was the most important. An older language and history close to Welsh and Breton; physical isolation in difficult terrain with poor communications; a different and older religious tradition; a rich mythology of separateness – these all played their parts, but it was tin, which England needed but could not get anywhere else, that guaranteed Cornwall's singular pattern of development. It has been calculated that at the end of the Middle Ages something like one in ten of the adult population was employed directly or indirectly in the tin industry in Cornwall.

The *Black Prince's Register* throws some light on the scope of the industry at that time. It records one Abraham the Tinner as employing three hundred men in a series of seven works running up the Fowey valley to Smallacombe, on Bodmin Moor. Abraham also stated that his grandfather had held the works before him, which suggests that the moor's heartland was an important site in the tin trade which flourished before the ravages of the Black Death.

Earlier documentary evidence is slight before the twelfth century. The Venerable Bede, writing in the early years of the eighth century, managed to shed more light on the Dark Ages than anyone else 'up-country'. But on the subject of tin he is remote and silent except for one doubtful word, *plumbum*, which appears in his list of British metals. This normally means 'lead', but at that period, used with the adjective 'white', it meant 'tin'. Possibly Bede intended to record white and black lead together, i.e. tin and lead. If he was referring to tin in Britain, then it would have come from Devon or Cornwall, but this is a very slight piece of evidence.

The archaeological clues

are a little more informative. Stream-works have produced enough tenth-century Saxon coins to convince us that the industry was active from early in that century. The Saxon silver hoard found in an old stream-work at Trewhiddle near St Austell must bear the same implication. But there is no mention of tin production in Domesday Book although other types of mine in other districts are accounted for. (It should be said, though, that today we have become accustomed to finding Domesday's information rather less complete than was once thought.) Some seventy years after Domesday, the Pipe Roll of 1155 – 56 records the taxes imposed on a flourishing and expanding tin industry, with more tin being produced in west Devon than Cornwall. In the first eleven years of the tax returns in the Pipe Rolls, output increased nearly five-fold. Prospectors were probably moving west to the richer Cornish gravels.

William de Wrotham Organizes the Stannaries

During the reigns of Richard I and John, the tinners suffered from the royal need for money, as did most of the population. But this also meant that those who could provide the money could bargain. In 1198 Hubert Walter, the Royal Justiciar, sent a particularly competent official to reorganize the mines, William de Wrotham. His mission was an immediate and enormous financial success for the Crown. William not only increased the duty on tin, he brought order by standardizing the weight of the ingots, and set up an effective staff to collect the tax and enforce Stannary Law.

The Stannaries were a very special example of processes that could be observed throughout society. By the beginning of the thirteenth century, feudal restrictions had tightened up to the point where professions outside the simple rural feudal hierarchy needed protection and immunity from the normal courts of the feudal lords. Such privileges could be obtained by corporate bodies, e.g. towns, guilds and universities, if they could raise enough money to tempt needy governments and embarrassed lords, and then the new freedoms would be embodied in charters. When the law courts began to insist that a villein's goods were the property of his lord, the professional tinner had to get free of the taint of villeinage and the lord's court.

From the government's point of view chartering a corporate body had very important advantages. A fixed income (subject only to upward revision) was substituted for an erratic one that was difficult and expensive to collect. The costs of collection and administration would be shed. Behind all the charters granted in this period we can detect bargaining for mutual advantage. The great granters of charters, King Richard I and King John, were always desperately in need of cash.

The working tinner got what he most needed when the Charter of the Stannaries was granted by John in 1201. He became exempt from the jurisdiction of all courts other than the Stannaries, which had complete civil and criminal power over him, apart from pleas of the Crown. His ancient 'customs' were preserved, and his law could be added to or amended in the Tinners' Convocation, which was the Stannary Parliament. Perhaps the most essential custom, that he should be able to carry out the necessary prospecting side of his work, was guaranteed by reaffirming the ancient right of free 'bounding'. This permitted him to search for tin on any unenclosed land, and to mark out his claim by turves at its corners, and to carry out other necessary practices of his trade, such as diverting watercourses. By way of compensation for the bounding, the lord of the soil that he worked was entitled to one-fifteenth of the tin raised.

There were four Stannaries in Cornwall: Foweymore, roughly what is now less happily called Bodmin Moor; Blackmore, Hensbarrow, and the St Austell area; Tywarnhaile, St Agnes, Redruth, Truro, and the country in between; and Penwith and Kerrier in the far west. Each had its court administering civil and criminal justice and this was subject only to the overall jurisdiction of the Warden of the Stannaries' court.

De Wrotham identified four sorts of working tinners, each with their own laws: diggers, black (i.e. unsmelted) tin buyers, smelters, and tin merchants. His success in multiplying the income from the Stannaries was not simply because he increased the severity of the laws, but also because he set up an effective staff to collect the money. All white tin in its now standard-size blocks had to be brought to one of the coinage towns and assayed and stamped before being offered for sale. This could only be done at the regular 'coinages', originally twice a year at each of the four Stannary towns, Liskeard, Lostwithiel, Truro and Helston. The name 'coinage' was derived from the French *coin* or 'corner', since a corner was cut from each ingot to test it for purity before stamping it.

The income from tin varied with production, but the most needy governments could commute it for a fixed amount by letting the collection out to a 'farmer' (the English equivalent of the Biblical publican) for a lump sum, and this was done from time to time. Another right the Crown reserved to itself was the right of pre-emption, or first refusal of tin offered for sale. Similarly, when the Royal need was desperate, this right could be farmed too.

The duty at coinage, in Cornwall forty shillings per thousandweight, was the chief source of revenue. By contrast, the duty on exported tin was only five shillings (later ten), apparently to discourage smuggling; but in practice wholesale smuggling went on, and special small illegal bars were produced to make this easier.

The historian Dr John Hatcher has lifted a corner of the veil on the mixture of criminality and enterprise in Cornwall's medieval tin-trade. He cites the case of Michael Trenewith, who combined moneylending on a large scale with 'smuggling, wrecking, fraud and coercion'. According to the *Black Prince's Register,* he was owed upwards of three hundred pounds, which was almost certainly a gross underestimate. He worked with local pewterers, illegally evading duty by selling to them direct. In 1342, along with half a dozen confederates, he was accused of seizing tin works by force and making the tinners work for one halfpenny per day when they were currently producing tin worth 20 pence. Among his debtors were some of the leading figures in the county.

Few working tinners ever presented tin at the coinage. They appear to have disposed of it earlier, either because smelting costs were too high for them, or because the burdens of waiting for coinage and the cost of transporting the tin were not easily borne, or, most often, they had borrowed from dealers or merchants, and pledged the tin in advance against cash loans. It was not uncommon for moneylenders to acquire and run tinworks when the tinner defaulted on his debt. As in most medieval industries of any scale, or which required capital for development work before any pay-off (notably cloth manufacture), control tended to pass from the working craftsman to the dealer or merchant who could advance money.

In the fifteenth century the dominance of relatively few, very rich men seemed to pass away as they were replaced by a more numerous group of men with more modest fortunes. This change is very similar to what was happening in the wool trade at the same time. A consequence of this appears to be that the working tinner was less often in hock to the merchant. Even if he could only stay as a wage labourer but keep out of debt, the increase in wages that came about after the Black Death would enable him to do rather better than his predecessors. Nevertheless tinners' working conditions were notoriously poor, and with the technological changes that occurred late in the Middle Ages they grew worse.

But always there was the gambling element. As long as tin mining lasted there was the hope of 'striking it rich', but with this went the chance of losing everything, and falling into hopeless debt. Not only did the moneylenders resort to violence in their attempts to recover bad debts, even Duchy officials engaged in protection rackets. Gang warfare, well known up-country, seems to have been prevalent in Cornwall too. A hundred years later Carew in his *Survey* described the usury and system of truck payment operating against the working tinner of his time.

Regrettable though it may be, these were already long-established practices in an always precarious industry.

CORNISH CASTLES Under William's Norman settlement

of the land, the Count of Mortain was overlord and by far the biggest landholder in Cornwall. He secured the two main routes in and out of the county by two castles, Dunheved (later Launceston) and Trematon on the southern route near Saltash. A good deal still remains of the castle at Launceston, and even parts of the town wall. It is the only walled town Cornwall has ever possessed, and most of the Southgate is still astride the road with the customary two gates, one large and one small, over the road and footpath. The Count established his own market at Dunheved, ruining the market of the Priory nearby, and another at Trematon which had the same effect on the Priory at St Germans.

The Norman rulers needed castles to defend their lands following the Conquest, and in time the lesser lord came to build their own. The Pomerays built one at Tregony, the Cardinhams at Cardinham. From what remains of the latter today it appears to have been a modest earthwork motte and bailey. Most contemporary castles seem to have started in that way, even the other

Top: Launceston is the only walled town in Cornwall, and much of the old line of the fortifications can still be traced.
Above: Of the many prisoners held in Launceston Castle, George Fox, the Quaker, was one of the most notable, Public hangings were carried out on the green slopes below the castle until 1821.
Left: Borlase has here exercised his imagination – though not excessively – to show Launceston as a fortified castle-town. From an engraving in *Antiquities* (1769).

Left: Restormel, one of Cornwall's finest castles, was begun in about 1200 by Robert de Cardinham who was responsible for the sturdy shell-keep with its crenellations and sentry walk.

Above: Seen from the air, the strength and simplicity of Restormel are revealed. The substantial gate house is on the right of the keep, and the chapel opposite.

Cardinham castle, Restormel, which is still quite majestic.

Robert de Cardinham is credited with constructing the great circular shell-keep of Restormel in about 1200. Its walls are nine feet thick and about twenty-seven feet high, carrying a sentry walk and crenellations. The domestic rooms were immediately inside the wall, and at first were made of timber; they were replaced by stone rooms in the time of Richard, Earl of Cornwall, which considerably improved the domestic accommodation. Wider windows were added, the chapel was built out over the ditch, and a new gate house was installed. The flat ground to the west, where visitors usually come from the car park, is the site of the old bailey.

When the Duchy of Cornwall was created in 1337, the keep contained a hall, three chambers and three upper chambers, and there were more rooms in the bailey to cater for staff and others. Even in ruins Restormel was so well sited that, centuries later in the Civil War, it still proved formidable.

Above: Restormel Castle, which continued to prove its worth in the Civil War.
Below: Borlase's engraving of Tintagel Castle indicates that rather more was standing in the 1760s than is visible today, though the view is still recognizable. From *Antiquities* (1769).

Trematon, also a shell-keep, is similar to Restormel and Launceston, and its thirteenth-century gate house remains complete. Totnes, nearby in Devon, is of a similar design.

There was one other major Cornish castle, Tintagel, which had been begun by Reginald, Earl of Cornwall, in about 1140. This Richard acquired by purchase, so completing his hand. Tintagel has the most dramatic site of all, with the sea separating the outer bailey from the rest of the castle, which can now be reached only by a narrow footbridge. In 1538, commenting on the damage wrought by the sea, the antiquary John Leland said: 'The residue of the buildings of this castle be sore weather beaten... belike it had three wards, but two be worn away by the gulping in of the sea insomuch that it has made almost an isle...'

In the anarchy of Stephen's reign, unauthorized 'adulterine' castles sprang up all over the country. Henry I with characteristic vigour set about demolishing them when he succeeded to the throne. It has been suggested that Kilkhampton Castle was one of these, and that Truro Castle disappeared so soon because it also was adulterine. The site of the castle long remained empty, and was called the 'castle fee'.

Cornwall has another group of castles and fortifications which, curiously, were brought into being by and for the use of gunpowder, although most authorities say that gunpowder made them obsolete. In 1547 French raiders burned Fowey, and the gallant wife of Thomas Treffry, in her husband's absence, took in the townsfolk to her house,

Tintagel Castle, occupying a highly dramatic site, was begun in about 1140 by Reginald, Earl of Cornwall. When Henry Ill's brother Richard (1209–72) was Earl, the two mainland wards were built with a bridge connecting them to the original inner ward around the hall.

Place, and held it against the French. After this the two simple blockhouses guarding the harbour were built, and a chain was slung between them that could be raised to close the entrance.

Henry VIII, in expectation of attack from France, decided to fortify the shores in east Kent and Sussex, and the Carrick Roads which could have proved a superb base for any invading French army to seize. To

Left: Place House, Padstow, built on the site of monastic ruins. The house is still in the hands of the descendents of Nicholas Prideaux, the Steward of the last Prior of Bodmin. Much of the Reformation house remains, embellished in the eighteenth and early nineteenth centuries in the 'Gothic' style. The illustration is from an engraving in *Views in Devonshire & Cornwall* with original drawings by Thomas Allom and W. H. Bartlett (1832).
Below left: The splendid setting of St Mawes Castle on top of the cliffs lends a touch of romance to what is little more than a complex gun-platform, ordered by Henry VIII as a strongpoint to guard the Carrick Roads. From an engraving in *Views* (1832).
Below: Castles similar to St Mawes were built at Pendennis and on the flat shores of Kent; this aerial view brings out the innate superiority of the Cornish sites.

do this he added to the defences at Fowey by strengthening St Catherine's Fort, and built castles at Pendennis and St Mawes which are similar in design to those installed in Kent on the flat foreshore from Sandown to Deal and Walmer, and at Camber in Sussex. These castles were placed to carry as heavy a concentration of big guns as possible, on almost solid round bastions with casements that offered a very small target but a wide field of fire which could catch any approaching enemy with cross-fire. The castles themselves could be very heavily defended by lighter guns and muskets, massed at key points and firing through small embrasures. Disposed on rocky cliffs, Pendennis and St Mawes are much more pleasing, and certainly better finished in more attractive stone, than their south-eastern counterparts.

In the Civil War Grenville's Royalists demonstrated the devastating effect that a few ships could have on the region when the Scillies were in enemy hands. Once Blake had captured the islands, the fortress and gun platform known as Cromwell's Castle replaced the earlier ruined fort called King Charles's Castle. About the same time it was deemed advisable to strengthen the defences of St Michael's Mount.

St Michael's Mount

Some archaeologists think that St Michael's Mount is the isle of Ictis, the tin island of classical literature, and romantic imagination has peopled it with visiting Phoenicians in the Iron Age. What is certain is that the Middle Ages found its topography ideal for a monastic site – almost cut-off from the wicked world by sea, but with limited access at low tide for necessities which were brought from the mainland along a causeway.

By the end of the fifth century it appears to have been a shrine or a place of visions, and it has

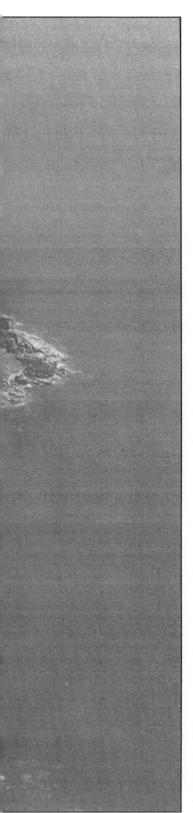

been suggested that there was a Celtic monastery there. This was replaced in 1044 by a cell of Benedictine monks from the monastery on the similar island of Mont St Michel off the Breton coast. Part of the early church may survive in the form of a crypt found under the chapel in the eighteenth century, but this is no longer accessible. Since the monastery was the daughter house of a foreign foundation, it was taken over in Henry VI's Dissolution of the Alien Priories and granted to the Brigittine nuns of Syon Abbey.

After the building and rebuilding of the monastery, and the addition of fortifications from time to time, and despite the further addition of the harbour, the Mount must still have lived up to its old Latin name, St Michael *in periculo maris* (St Michael in peril of the sea). It remained not much more than an almost bare rock with a few buildings until the late nineteenth century when it, like so many places on the southern shores of west Cornwall, was planted up in sub-tropical fashion. But even after the Second World War there was a sharp reminder that the rock was still essentially what it always had been when the old battleship HMS *Warspite*, on its way to the breaker's yard, slipped its tow and wrecked itself on the Mount, which became again a place of popular pilgrimage as long as the *Warspite* stayed there. There is still a beacon on the chapel tower roof, known as St Michael's Chair. Much medieval fabric is incorporated in the buildings, but most of it has been altered out of recognition. The old refectory is now the Chevy Chase Room because it carries a fascinating plaster frieze of hunting scenes.

Ownership passed to the St Aubyn family late in the seventeenth century, and the attractive additions and alterations from then on are due to the personal interest of various members of the family, including at least one trained architect. Since 1954 the island has been owned by the National Trust.

Left: St Michael's Mount, where Benedictine monks from the similar island of Mont St Michel, Brittany, established themselves in 1044.

Below: The Mount, as seen by Borlase. For all his exaggeration of its height, the site was much more rugged than it appears today. From *Antiquities* (1769).

THE DUCHY OF CORNWALL

It is a fond and popular illusion that the County of Cornwall *is* the Duchy. In fact the Duchy consists of estates which in Cornwall occupy a good deal less than the whole county but which include other substantial areas of land beyond the Tamar. Today this conglomeration has become virtually inalienable as the permanent endowment of the heir to the throne. The Duchy's origins go back to the anarchy of the twelfth century and its predecessor, the Earldom of Cornwall, the lands of which form the core of the modern Duchy.

Reginald, one of Henry I's numerous illegitimate sons, and half-brother of the Empress Matilda, assumed the title of Earl of Cornwall, but Stephen (reigned 1135–54) brought an army into Cornwall, recovered the castles, and awarded the Earldom to Count Alan of Brittany.

Matilda's son, who came to the throne as Henry II (reigned 1154–89), confirmed Reginald as Earl of Cornwall. Richard I (reigned 1189–99) intended to confirm the Earldom on his brother, John, but since he was only eight when it became vacant by Reginald's death, John never held the title himself. Instead he granted the County of Cornwall to his second son, Richard, along with the Stannaries, and made him Earl of Cornwall.

Eventually, in 1257, Richard became King of the Romans, having distributed enough bribes among the voters to secure his election, but he failed to make anything material from this empty title. By contrast, he took more personal interest in Cornwall than the other Earls. He improved Dunheved Castle, and acquired Tintagel, Restormel and Trematon.

He was succeeded as Earl by his son Edmund, who was also active in Cornwall. From his period are the stone rooms that make the living quarters inside Restormel Castle. Previously there had been only timber rooms, much less suitable for an important residence. After Edmund, the Cornish castles were neglected, and the Earldom for a time had the indignity of being conferred on Piers Gaveston, favourite and foster-brother of Edward II.

A major change came after the last Earl, John, died in 1336 without heirs. In the following year Edward the Black Prince was made Duke of Cornwall, the first Duke in England, and the lands were made the property of the monarch's first-born son.

The Duchy Palace at Lostwithiel

Under Earl Edmund, Lostwithiel had developed as the centre of his Cornish estates. With the lowest bridge across the Fowey, it became an important port as mining developed in Foweymore and Blackmore. Guarded by the powerful Restormel above it, it acquired an importance that is difficult to detect in the present town, although pieces of the Middle Ages are to be found half-hidden in its buildings, particularly in the conglomeration known as the Duchy Palace (inaccurately, since no Duke, or Earl, stayed there).

The buildings served as the administrative centre of the Duchy lands in the South-West, as the County Court and as the offices for the coinage. Part of the powerful privilege of the medieval Duchy was the right to appoint the Sheriff, and this office was normally performed by the Duke's Steward, who would have been resident in Lostwithiel. The Duke had the perquisites of the Shire Court and of eight and a half of the nine 'Hundred' courts. (A Hundred was the old local governmental division within the shire.) The knights of the shire (MPs) were elected here and this custom remained until the Great Reform Act.

As well as the staff required for the management of such enormous estates there were extra officials such as the Havenor, who exercised the Duke's rights over the seas and the ports, including customs, right of wreck, and the prise of wine (the royal entitlement to one tun, of about 250 gallons, of wine carried before the mast and one abaft the mast; the prize usually amounted to a duty of about 65½ per cent). There were also the Constables of the castles, and the Feodary, who exercised the Duke's feudal rights, including such sources of profit as rents from the Court of Wards (income from the property of heirs while they were under-age).

The buildings contained accommodation for Duchy officials, the weighing-house and blowing-house for the coinage, storage for tin and such other items as the wine from the prise, and shops under the Great Hall. Here too was housed the abominable Stannary prison. Some of this can be traced today, and part of the charm of Lostwithiel is not only the medieval bridge and Duchy Palace that we know about, but the small pieces of work from those times that greet us unawares as we walk around the town.

Next to the Great Hall, and in part of its former space, are some eighteenth-century buildings which have iron bars to the top-floor windows; clearly these upper rooms replaced the older, decayed prison, heavily damaged in the Civil War. To the west of the Great Hall are buildings incorporating fragments of older work: possibly these were Stannary buildings (Smelting House Lane is nearby), and possibly they included the nineteenth-century slaughterhouse, when Lostwithiel exported large quantities of meat to London.

The building that survives best from medieval Lostwithiel is the Convocation Hall. Presumably it was used for the Tinners' Parliament (Convocation) when the Great Hall fell into decay. The upper floor is now the Masonic Hall, but it contains much of the original work.

Under Queen Elizabeth I, who was always chronically short of money, some Cornish manors of the Duchy were sold. This was illegal since no parts of the Duchy may be alienated. James I seized them back. Under Cromwell the Duchy was abolished, but at the Restoration it came back into being.

Although, in modern times, Prince Charles needed to 'await his Mother's pleasure' before being invested Prince of Wales, he was born Duke of Cornwall. In the 1970s, after almost fifty years, the Duke revived for the last time the ancient medieval practice whereby his feudal tenants met him at Launceston to pay their rents. These bore the mark of antiquity: a brace of white whippets, a pair of gloves, a deerskin cloak, a pound of cummin (a plant resembling fennel) and a hundred shillings of blanched silver. Cupro-nickel would not do and the shillings had to be specially struck. Sadly, recent local government changes mean that the ceremony will never be held again.

Convocation Hall, Lostwithiel. Now the Masonic Lodge, this is probably the site of the so-called Duchy Palace, where the Tinners' Parliament met. The title is not strictly accurate since there is no record of any Earl or Duke staying there. When they came to the town they used nearby Restormel.

CORNISH CHURCHES

The Age of the Saints had left Cornwall in some sense a Christian land, if still, at the beginning of the tenth century, outside the orbit of the Catholic Church as understood by Rome. By that time, in spite of centuries of religious and economic vandalism, the stone crosses, long a prominent feature of the landscape, had proliferated. As we have seen, some of the early ones with memorial inscriptions were grave stones. Some may be heathen standing stones, taken over and Christianized by missionaries such as St Sampson. Some seem to have marked moorland tracks; some were on property boundaries, and may have served the same function as the crosses drawn on Anglo-Saxon boundary charters – to warn of the curse on would-be violators.

The Church of St Germans, once the Cathedral of Cornwall, became the church of an Augustinian order of canons in the twelfth century. The west doorway, of seven receding orders, is the pride of Cornish church architecture. The twin west towers belong to the Norman plan, but the upper stage of the northern tower was modified in the thirteenth century to become an octagon. From an engraving by Norden.

The great Cornish scholar Charles Henderson suggested that many Cornish churches began as preaching crosses, set up in round or oval enclosures that became graveyards when the churches were built.

Very early churches are difficult to find in Cornwall, although Norman work, at least in fragments, is plentiful. St Piran-in-the-Sands, near Perranzabuloe (which means the same thing), seems to have been an oratory built in the sixth or seventh century: the cell or chapel of a Dark Age saint. It is the oldest church in Devon and Cornwall. Nothing now stands from any church that we could call Saxon, although there are some standing stones with Anglo-Saxon inscriptions, such as that in the churchyard at Lanteglos-by-Camelford.

From the Norman period, the picture is very different. The finest Norman work is at St Germans, where a large part of the church of the Augustinian canons still survives. They took over the site of the old Cathedral of the Cornish Diocese, amalgamated with Crediton in 1050 to form the new See of Exeter. The present church retains much of the late Norman work, for the canons only came about a century after the end of the Cornish See. The west doorway, of seven receding orders, is the pride of Cornish churches. St Germans also has an unusual western façade, with two square towers, the northern of which became a thirteenth-century octagon.

None of the Norman parish churches can compare with St Germans, but Pevsner suggests that about 140 churches in Cornwall show some Norman work. One of the most surprising is St Breward. At the summit of a long, steep climb up the edge of the moor is what claims to be the highest church in England. It is almost the last building in the village. The north aisle is Norman, with five unequal piers, and unequal arcades, mostly of local moorstone although some of the stone appears to have come from much further afield. It is difficult to find a reason, with such a profusion of moorstone nearby, why huge rocks should have been hauled up what then must have been an almost impossible road. The old Norman font may have been reconstituted from fragments, and there are hints that originally the church was cruciform.

Pevsner counted 111 Norman fonts in Cornwall. They range from rustic to elegant. One of the best is at Bodmin, and another very good one, which could have come from the same mason, is in the parish church of Roche. Altogether the amount of parish church building in Cornwall to survive from the Early English and Decorated periods (1180–1350) is relatively slight because of the enormous building and rebuilding that went on in the fifteenth century. Perhaps the best example of what so many of them must have been like before this 'Great Rebuilding' is St Anthony-in-Roseland. There are very few Cornish spires, and most of them are from the fifteenth century: St Anthony's spire, over the crossing tower, is of timber and lead.

Medieval Building Patterns

Since so much has survived from the fifteenth century, Pevsner was able to suggest that something like three-quarters of the churches in Cornwall belong to three or four set types which were established by 1400. These types are found in Devon also, and any reader interested in medieval churches has an excellent opportunity in the South-West to identify and compare the various patterns.

External variations come partly from the use of local stone, and more so from an exuberance in external decoration which arrived in about 1460. St Mary Magdalene at Launceston is perhaps the supreme example of this; amazingly, the stone,

Church and churchyard at Altarnun, on the northern edge of Bodmin Moor. This is probably one of the best churches for decorative woodwork in the South-West. The Celtic cross in the churchyard may have been a preaching cross from the days before the church was built.

Above left: Much of the carving in church interiors reveals folk art of great vigour and quality, like this Norman head on the font bowl at Altarnun (the name means the 'altar of St Non').
Above right: One of the 79 carved wooden bench-ends at Altarnun, dating from just before the Reformation. This one appears to be a sword dancer.

so richly decorated, is intractable granite. Notable features of Cornish churches of the fifteenth century are waggon roofs, the woodwork of bench-ends (e.g. Altarnun) and screens (e.g. St Buryan). The abundance of first-class slate in the county has encouraged local enterprise in making memorials, producing every degree of variation from the rustic, primitive effigies in the tiny churchyard of St Enedoc, preserved by the sands, to the remarkable high-relief carvings at St Tudy.

Not very much wall-painting survives, but as well as traditional St Christophers with the Christ Child (e.g. Breage) there are several examples of what used to be thought of as Christ and the Trades, which are now interpreted as a

warning to Sabbath-breakers; the tools for work wrongly done on the Sabbath are displayed around the crucified Christ. Again, Breage is probably the best of the four Cornish examples.

For stained glass surviving from before the Reformation, St Neot is unequalled. The east window in the south wall has a wonderful boisterous life of Noah, starting from his cutting down the trees and building the ark, and showing him as he traditionally was, a drunkard, rolling beer barrels up into an ark that looks remarkably like a fifteenth-century ship.

The Middle Ages seem to have lasted late in Cornwall. Their passing, in terms of church architecture, is marked by the Restoration church dedicated to

Charles King and Martyr in Falmouth, with its splendid Ionic columns and Classical interior in what, viewed from the exterior, is in some ways still a parish church in the late medieval tradition.

As well as its profusion of crosses, Cornwall is rich in other aids for medieval wayfarers. Only one Cornish bridge seems to have had a chapel on it: Looe. The bridge at Wadebridge was built by John Lovibond, a fifteenth-century vicar of Egloshayle across the river. It seems to have been paid for by tolls on wool. It was thus 'built on wool', and a literal interpretation of the metaphor led to the popular theory that its piers were in fact founded on bales of wool, after a revelation to Lovibond in a dream. Alas, the same story appears

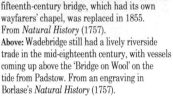

Top left: Remarkable high-relief carving in slate on a memorial at St Tudy Church, north of Bodmin. This aspect of Cornish church art deserves to be much better known than it is.
Top right: Looe has developed enormously since Borlase's engraving was made in the mid-eighteenth century, when East and West Looe were separate towns. The old

fifteenth-century bridge, which had its own wayfarers' chapel, was replaced in 1855. From *Natural History* (1757).
Above: Wadebridge still had a lively riverside trade in the mid-eighteenth century, with vessels coming up above the 'Bridge on Wool' on the tide from Padstow. From an engraving in Borlase's *Natural History* (1757).

elsewhere in England. Both the recent widening of the bridge, and earlier borings, showed that it was in fact based on solid bedrock. Fortunately, the widening was done with such skill as to preserve most of its medieval character, except of course for its narrowness.

Many holy wells survive. Those such as St Cleer, which have a building over them, seem to come from the late Middle Ages, but the unprotected ones are usually impossible to date and may well be from the Age of the Saints.

In the late fourteenth and early fifteenth century more wayside oratories and chapels were built. One of the most remarkable, which deserves to be known much better outside its own county, is Roche Rock.

Here a jagged pile of a particularly hard granite projects upwards while the softer surrounding rocks have been worn away. On the peak of the rock, and set firmly into it, are the ruins of a chapel; carved into the solid stone under the chapel floor is a hermit's cell. Other hermits had cells at Lostwithiel and Restormel, and another at Carn Brea is thought to have kept a lighthouse.

The cult of relics was as vigorous in Cornwall as elsewhere. The buoyant state of the market is indicated by the fact that monks from Laon in Brittany (those, mentioned earlier, who caused a riot by having the temerity to suggest, in Bodmin, that Arthur was dead) thought it worthwhile coming over to tout their relics around Cornwall and collect

money. When the monastery of St Petroc was reconstituted under the Rule of St Augustine, the saint's body was a powerful tourist attraction. One of the canons stole the body and took it to the continent but, happily, it was recovered, and, until the Reformation, the skull and bones were kept in a superb ivory casket that still survives.

Other popular shrines included St Michael's Mount, where the Celtic monks had been replaced by French Benedictines before the Norman Conquest. St Germans, Cornwall's cathedral city until 1043, had some local appeal, but nothing like that of St James of Compostela in Spain, one of the most popular shrines in Europe and not beyond the range of a hardy pilgrim from Cornwall.

Left: St Levan's holy well. Such wells are a prominent reminder of the visits of the early Celtic missionaries from Wales and Ireland.
Below far left: At Dupath a simple single-celled building stands by the spring.
Below: The structure on top of Roche Rock is an early fifteenth-century chapel. Under its floor, cut into the bedrock, is a hermit's cell. From an engraving in *Britannia Depicta, Cornwall* (1813).
Below left: In this modern photograph the top of the ruins of the chapel can just be seen on top of the Rock. Jan Tregeagle, the unjust steward, can be heard flying around the Rock at night and howling as he strives to carry out his appointed task of emptying Dozmary Pool.

MONASTERIES AND COUNTRY HOUSES

All the eight monastic establishments in post-Conquest Cornwall were dependent on houses outside the county, and, perhaps for that reason, none ever grew to rival the great Benedictine houses of the Midlands, or the Cistercian houses of the North. Nonetheless Cornwall had a number of tiny collegiate churches. St Endellion had four prebends, and still has three and a rector (having strangely got through the net at the Reformation). Nearby St Teath had a vicar

Cotehele, where the splendid Great Hall is the heart of one of the best Tudor houses in the country. Although there is stone of an earlier date in many of the walls, the dominant tone is of the early sixteenth century.

When the Dissolution of the Monasteries reached Cornwall, King Henry VIII had damaging evidence put together to justify his plundering of their property. As a result it is difficult to be sure how decayed and corrupt any particular house was at that time. Tywardreath appears to have been in a bad way and getting worse. St Germans, on the other hand, seems to have been quite well run.

The picture of the Cornish monasteries in their last years, and of their Dissolution, has been superbly told by A L Rowse in *Tudor Cornwall*.

It was not only the royal agents who cooked the evidence. Dissolution was rumoured long before it happened, and senior monks were sufficiently versed in the parable of the unjust steward to make friends with the mammonists of this world.

Dr Rowse has a telling picture of a meeting of canons at which their prior bribed them to seal certain documents unread, and to supply him with other sealed sheets of blank parchment so that he could forge leases and other papers.

The local gentry did very well out of the change, and so, to some extent, have we in the new buildings that have emerged from the spoils of and two prebends, and there seem to have been plenty more. It is a little difficult to envisage what kind of monastic establishment there was at Temple, when in 1340 the knights recorded a preceptor, one brother, two attendants and a chaplain. The college of Glasney (Penryn), founded by Bishop Bronescombe in about 1265 for a provost and twelve canons, has vanished virtually without trace. The little college founded in the sixteenth century by Thomasine Bonaventura at Week St Mary still exists, modified into a farmhouse. Much earlier in date, Launceston Priory has left a good Norman door which has been re-set as the front door of the White Hart Hotel.

Cotehele from the outside, admirably set off by its gardens which plunge down the valley to the Tamar. Set in the gardens, some seventy feet above the river, is a chapel built as a thanksgiving by Richard Edgcumbe who jumped from that point into the river to escape his enemies.

the priories. When the Eliots obtained the Priory of St Germans, they incorporated parts of it into a new family home, Port Eliot, where the great hall is the old refectory of the canons, and an undercroft survives from the thirteenth century. Sir Richard Edgcumbe built Mount Edgcumbe in the years after the Dissolution. Bombed and gutted during the Second World War, it has

arisen like a phoenix from the ashes when viewed from outside. The old family home, Cotehele, was little needed with such a grand new house available, and much of it survives unchanged from the later Middle Ages. It is difficult to think of another house of the period to rival it, anywhere in the country.

Cotehele, beside the Tamar, marks the full flowering, almost the

end of the medieval tradition. Its great open hall uses all its roof-timbers decoratively. Arch-braced, it has four tiers of interlaced wind-braces. All these, together with the purlins are moulded, giving a unique combination of delicacy and strength. The solar has an elegant little squint into the great hall, so that the ladies, having withdrawn, could keep an eye on developments after dinner.

Another charming survival from the end of the Middle Ages is Rialton where part of the medieval manor house, frequented by Prior Vivian from Bodmin, remains in the farmhouse.

A good proportion of the best country houses in Cornwall, underneath all the later accretions, additions and modifications, reveal signs of construction or reconstruction paid for by the spoils from church property. Fowey Place (the name is a close relative of the English 'palace') contains part of the Treffrys' post-Reformation house. Another Place, at Padstow, is also a fruit of the Dissolution. Nicholas Prideaux, the last Steward and relative by marriage of the last Prior of Bodmin, made a very astute agreement, and Place has remained in the family ever since.

The Arundells took an early interest in the dispersal of

In St Mawgan-in-Pydar is Lanherne, the house which in 1794 the Arundells gave to nuns fleeing from the French Revolution. The convent is still there in the house, which retains its Elizabethan front and is on the left of this engraving; beside it stands the church. In the garden is one of the most

monastic lands. At Lanherne, near St Columb Major, they built the house which still retains its Elizabethan front, and which they gave to nuns fleeing from the Revolution in France in 1794. It is still a convent. This branch of the Arundell family persisted in the Catholic faith, and there are hints that the Mass still may have been celebrated there during the persecutions of the late sixteenth century. In the nearby house where, according to local legend, the priests sheltered at that time, a Philip and Mary teston (shilling) which had been pierced and showed signs of having been worn on a chain round someone's neck, was found hidden on top of the wall-plate under the roof.

Even more remains to be seen of another Arundell house, Trerice near Newlyn East, built in the reign of Elizabeth I. At the time it must have been a satisfying and lively blend of old and new. It has a delightful pattern of curving gables, an enormous lattice hall window, and is altogether a brilliant decorative elaboration of what was essentially an old plan.

important Cornish crosses bearing a crucifixion, interlaced work and a Saxon inscription. The engraving is from *Views* (1832).

Menabilly, the house that the Rashleighs built about the end of Elizabeth's reign, has been extensively rebuilt at least twice. It is beautifully sited, and an excellent sample of how a family with wide economic interests, and an eye to opportunities such as the disposal of church property, could keep up with changes in ideas of domestic comfort and social life through the centuries. Menabilly is particularly famous for its connections with Daphne du Maurier, its gardens, and the Tristan stone at the gate of its East Lodge (mentioned earlier). The local town house of the Rashleighs is even earlier than Menabilly; this is now the Ship Inn, down the hill in Fowey, where a good deal of original work is visible.

Godolphin Hall, with material from the sixteenth century onwards, marks a new factor which stimulated the building of country houses: tin, and the fortune to be made by extracting it from the landowner's ground. The Godolphins had been in government service and dabbled in the property market, but as mineral discoveries moved westwards in the sixteenth century, it was the rich ore in their soil that made the family fortune. The house, not far from St Michael's Mount, seems to have had additions at many periods after it was first built in the sixteenth century. On the north side it has a Classical loggia on four stout Tuscan columns. This has been traditionally accepted as belonging to work of 1712; but Pevsner thought it was much earlier.

All the elements going to make early Cornish country houses combine at Lanhydrock, near Lostwithiel, to make a splendid house in a glorious setting. The site was originally monastic land. Sir Richard Robartes, a merchant of wool and tin from Truro, bought it in 1620. Much of the house was built before the Civil War and it was completed by 1651. The detached gate house was added later. In 1881 a disastrous fire swept

Right: Lanhydrock House, near Lostwithiel. Built by a successful merchant who bought the land in 1620, Lanhydrock suffered badly from a fire in 1881. It was rebuilt much as before, with new rooms added at the rear. From an engraving in *Views* (1832).
Below: The Long Gallery at Lanhydrock escaped the fire, and the original elaborate plaster ceiling remains intact.

through all except the north wing and the gate house. Fortunately the gallery, with its astonishing plasterwork ceiling, escaped the flames. The rest was rebuilt much as it was, and new rooms were added at the rear. Much of Lanhydrock's charm comes from the fact that it was occupied until recently by the family, a feeling which the National Trust, the present owners, has managed to maintain. Lady Robartes's desk looks

Left: The main entrance to Lanhydrock is through a porch at the top of the courtyard, opposite the gate house (behind the riders in the engraving).

Below: Until recently, when it passed to the National Trust, Lanhydrock was still the home of the original family, the Robartes. The Trust has preserved the atmosphere of the house, and Lady Robartes's desk remains ready as ever for tomorrow's work.

Above: Antony House, near Torpoint, was formerly the home of Richard Carew, author of the *Survey of Cornwall* (1601). This 'Palladian' version of the house has been attributed to James Gibbs (1682–1754). The main change since Borlase's engraving has been the addition of a porte-cochère. From *Natural History* (1757).

Right: Trelissick House, near Truro. This represents the most extreme development of the Classical revival in Cornwall. This illustration, and those that follow on these pages, is from an engraving in *Views in Devonshire & Cornwall* with original drawings by Thomas Allom and W. H. Bartlett (1832).

ready for tomorrow's work.

Probably the nearest that the Palladian style came to being 'naturalized' in Cornwall was at Antony House, near Torpoint. The use of red brick for the wings and the connecting walls to the corner pavilions strikes an unusual note in Cornwall. The house itself is of Pentewan stone. It has been attributed to James Gibbs, one of the most important architects of the time. In the early Victorian period a large pillared porte-cochère (porch into which a coach could be driven) was added in the centre to allow guests to dismount and keep dry in all weathers.

After Antony House, the important Cornish houses get involved in a 'battle of styles', caught between Gothic and Classical revivals. Caerhays Castle, above Veryan Bay, was designed by John Nash; it is

Above: Tregothnan House, near Truro. This house has a seventeenth-century core, but heavy mock-Tudor treatments in the nineteenth century have given it the appearance of a fantasy-house.
Below left: Morval, near Looe, one of the few Tudor E-shaped houses in Cornwall substantially to have survived despite later alterations.
Below: Place, at Fowey, is the house of the Treffry family. In the early nineteenth century much of the house was reworked in a romantic Gothic style, submerging the remains of the earlier post-Reformation house which in 1547 served as a fortress against the French.

castellated, with towers round and square, and is frankly romantic Gothic. It is seen at its best when the rhododendrons are out, adding exotic colour to the mature trees and ornamental lake that stand between the house and the cliff edge.

A few years later the Earl of Falmouth had the old family home, Tregothnan, encased in a fantasy of mock-Tudor, with a forest of tall moulded chimneys, octagonal turrets, mullioned and transomed windows, all of which look borrowed from the Norfolk of Henry VIII. The other side of the coin is illustrated by Trelissick, south of Truro, a Classical revival straight from the Athenian Acropolis. Its enormous Ionic portico with frieze and pediment almost smothers the more domestic façade. Its air of correctness seems a little pedantic in a Cornish garden where so many rare shrubs flourish.

Smaller Houses and Building Materials

The smaller houses have an interesting history of their own, and excellent historians. Any traveller in Cornwall with an interest in the county could hardly do better than take *The Cornishman's Home*, by V M and F J Chesher, and try to spot examples discussed in this remarkable book.

One of the best places to start looking is the Old Post Office at Tintagel. This is a late medieval house, and because of its quality is usually thought to be a small manor house. Its central hall is still open to the roof and it had a through passage between the hall and the domestic end. The large front-wall chimney seems to have been a status symbol in this area.

Many of the smaller medieval houses had three ground-floor rooms, and two main types can be distinguished. In one, the through passage was for man and beasts and at the lower end was a byre. In the other type the through passage (as in the Old Post Office at Tintagel) was not meant for animals, and instead of a byre had a service room or rooms.

Carew described in his *Survey* the more modest living conditions of Cornish husbandmen in the late sixteenth century: 'Walls of earth, low thatched roofs, few partitions, no planchings or glass windows, and scarcely any chimneys other than a hole in the wall to let out the smoke: their bed, straw and a blanket; as for sheets, so much linen cloth had not stepped over the narrow channel between them and Brittany.'

Carew also comments on the use of stone for building. He calls the mudstones 'quarry stone'. He divides this quarry stone into 'rough' (killas) and 'slate'. Moorstone was used for the finer work such as on windows and door jambs.

Slate, once the art of splitting it clean had been discovered, afforded such excellent roofing that it has been in use for centuries. Unlike the local granite it was extensively quarried, as is shown by the quarry at Delabole, near Tintagel, which has a circumference of four miles.

The quarrying of granite really began in the nineteenth century, and was usually done for public buildings. At De Lank Quarry on Bodmin Moor the base can still be seen on which Eddystone Lighthouse was erected before being built on its rock. Penryn granite was used for London Bridge and other Thames bridges. As roads became improved and tarmacadamized, vast quantities of kerbstones were needed, and this helped to make the quarries prosperous for some time. Very little quarrying takes place now: as techniques for making hard, durable concrete improved, so cheap substitutes were manufactured near where they were to be installed, and the demand for granite kerbs declined.

Top left: The Old Post Office, Tintagel, is a medieval house based on a hall in the centre open to the roof, with a through passage at one end separating the hall from the service end, and private rooms at the opposite end. The enormous fireplace on the front wall by the door was possibly for social display, and may have been a later insertion.

Top right: Edmonton, an industrial village built for the workers at Camel Quarry. The village was built as a single rectangle with all the twenty-four four-roomed cottages facing into the court which had a common pump in the centre. Earth closets at the rear were given a back lane for access. Across one end was a chapel, and at the other a thirteen-roomed 'Count House', for the manager and his office.

Above: Delabole Quarry is alleged to be the largest man-made hole in the ground in England. A number of smaller quarries have run together in the course of time and the circuit of the quarry is now four miles. Delabole slate is of an exceptionally high quality, splits very thinly and cleanly for roofing slates, and offers a very regular silky slate for memorials. In recent years, ground slate powder has been in some demand for such products as paint, roofing felt and recording discs.

TOWNS AND FISHING PORTS

In Cornwall villages had always been rare and larger settlements very few, and the Cornish seemed extraordinarily reluctant to live in towns during the Middle Ages. There were no boroughs recorded in Cornwall in Domesday Book, although perhaps it might reasonably have called Bodmin a town, for there the canons had sixty-eight houses and a market. There were probably five other markets in the county.

In the Lay Subsidy Rolls of 1327, two-thirds of the names in some of the towns were foreign, not Cornish. But Domesday shows that the markets were being guarded by their landlords as sources of income. As far as we can see, virtually all the Cornish towns in the Middle Ages were the result of initiatives taken by landlords who saw that they would do well if they were able to exchange low agricultural rents for the higher yields of urban properties. As we saw earlier, monarchs in need of cash were ready to grant charters, and so there was no real obstacle to founding a town provided people could be persuaded in sufficient numbers to uproot themselves and move to the chosen site.

The outstanding Cornish historian Charles Henderson has left us much material and commentary on Cornish medieval towns and their origins in his *Essays in Cornish History*. He pointed out how the long estuaries pushed the lowest bridging points of the rivers far inland. In such a position a town could be the market centre for a large hinterland as well as a convenient sea port. He cited as examples Truro, Tregony, Helston, Lostwithiel and Penryn. But silting, especially as streamworks developed on all the main rivers of the county, created great trouble. Tregony had to abandon any pretensions as a port in the seventeenth century, when an attempt to tow a ship up to the quay

failed. Grampound was up higher and also failed as a port, but it remained a halt with a great bridge across the river; in this way it performed a similar function to Michell or Camelford which were sited on main roads to the north.

At Grampound the land on either side of the river was in the manor of Tybesta, which was in the hands of the Earl of Cornwall. In 1332 it received a charter which granted the burgesses extensive rights. They were to be free of toll throughout Cornwall, to have a Gild Merchant (traders' association), the right to

In the ancient town of Truro, on the south aisle of the old parish Church of St Mary, the Victorian architect J. L. Pearson built a cathedral wholeheartedly in the Early English pointed Gothic style, complete with spires. As the seat of the diocese of Cornwall, it had to have a copper roof which has weathered a livid green. Begun in 1890 and completed in 1910, the Cathedral now dominates the surrounding streets which contain some fine Georgian houses.

Above: Mevagissey. In its great days as a fishing port it was known as 'Fishy Gissy'. There could scarcely be a better example of how closely a town can grow around its harbour.
Left: Comparison with the recent photograph shows how Mevagissey has also grown outwards, covering the surrounding hills with streets and houses. This engraving, from *Britannia Depicta, Cornwall,* was published in 1813.
Top right: Mousehole is a fishing town with a tiny harbour etched into the stone country. Quintessentially Cornish, it has squeezed into existence between fields made by prehistoric man and the surrounding ocean.
Above right: Polperro. Already a town tumbling down the hillside to its little harbour in 1813, its people and houses have greatly multiplied since this engraving was made for *Britannia Depicta.*
Right: Mullion Cove, c. 1880. At top left is the capstan for the lifeboat which was there from 1867 until 1908.

hang thieves taken within the borough, two annual fairs and a weekly market. The courts of the Hundred (i.e. the Sheriff's Court for freemen) were to be held in the borough, which guaranteed the town a considerable degree of freedom from outside interference.

Fishing Ports

The siting of Cornish fishing ports was easier to determine than the most advantageous place to build a town. Where the cliffs break, and boats can get in and out with some sort of haven, fishermen have always been prepared to take the risk. Henderson lists as typical ports Mousehole, Looe, Marazion, Fowey, St Mawes, Saltash and Padstow. There are many more, and some of the very tiny coves, scarcely recognizable as fishing ports today, are not the least interesting.

There is little evidence of a Cornish sea-fishing industry in the early Middle Ages, and fishing ports appear late in the Cornish landscape. Polperro and Port Isaac are mentioned in the first half of the fourteenth century, but the expansion of fishing seems to have occurred later, possibly as a means of avoiding the economic depression which elsewhere followed the Black Death. Enormous imports of salt indicate that fish was being preserved on a rapidly increasing scale before it was exported along the coast and abroad.

In the older ports much of the activity was concentrated around the fishermen's houses on the quayside. Underneath the living quarters the ground floor was open and served as a fish cellar. In the bigger establishments these were grouped around the sides of a courtyard, and dignified by the name of 'fish palace'. Here the great staple for centuries of the Cornish fisheries – the pilchard – was salted, packed in barrels, and pressed. For long the great export market for pilchards was to be found in the Mediterranean Catholic countries. A valuable by-

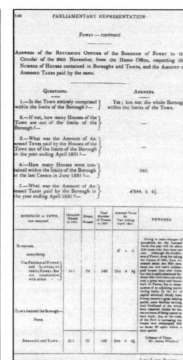

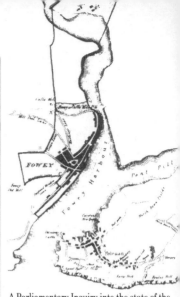

A Parliamentary Inquiry into the state of the hundred smallest boroughs was one precursor of the Great Reform Bill, and has left this map of 1831 and report on Fowey. A great deal of building has been accomplished since that time on both sides of the harbour, in Polruan and Bodinnick as well as in Fowey itself. The superb quality of the harbour, sheltering in the long-drowned valley, comes out very clearly in the map.

product, the train oil expressed from the fish, helped to pay the overheads.

Carew recognized the supremacy of the pilchard in Cornwall, a recent phenomenon in his time: 'But the least fish in bigness, the greatest for gain, and most in number, is the pilchard.' The pilchard usually came in great shoals into Cornish waters after the harvest, which encouraged a lot of people to take up fishing as a part-time occupation.

The two chief ways of catching pilchards were by seining or drifting. Already in Carew's time there was bad feeling between the seiners and the drifters. The seiners complained that the drift-nets (which caught the fish by the gills) damaged the fish, and thereby harmed the reputation of Cornish pilchards, and also frightened the shoals away from the shallows.

Seining was carried out by three or four boats, each crewed by about six men. They surrounded the shoal in the shallows, under the direction of a man on the cliff-top, the 'huer' or 'balker', who used a special

Left: Huer's house, Newquay. From his look-out position on top of the cliff, the huer signalled the arrival of a shoal to the seine fishermen in the water below, and helped them to manoeuvre their nets around it.

Below: Fishing exhibition at St Ives in 1893, with fishermen displaying their catch on the beach. These appear to be competition winners and the catch is impressive.

Above: A sight that has, alas, gone. This photograph proves that the pilchard could still arrive in force off St Ives in 1905.

set of signals, and brought the full net to land. The best-known of the surviving huer's houses today is the one at Newquay, an attractive whitewashed chapel-like structure with a small watchtower.

Much of the exported tin, fish, cloth, slate and other Cornish produce was carried in Cornish vessels. In addition, a growing ship-building trade in the little Cornish ports accounted for an impressive output of Cornish boats exported in the late fifteenth century. Design, size and construction varied according to the types of fish being sought and to conditions on the coast. At St Ives and nearby ports, for instance, most of the fishing boats were double-ended to cope with the short-breaking waves of the bay. Around the Lizard, transom sterns appeared again. The shallow sandy beaches that suited the seiners have more recently proved ideal for family seaside holidays, so encouraging the development of many of the fishing ports into holiday resorts.

Wreckers and Pirates

The popular picture of eighteenth-century Cornishmen shows them as enthusiastic smugglers and wreckers, or worse, pirates. Behind the exaggeration lies the undoubted fact that trade had existed long before customs duties, and every increase in duty encouraged and increased the profitability of smuggling. It has been estimated that in 1770 the loss to the Revenue amounted to £150,000. It had become almost an economic necessity for tinners near the coast to resort to smuggling in times of distress. An allied problem was that the penalties of being caught all too easily led men in danger of discovery to turn to violence. Corruption spread. Magistrates, who were themselves involved, turned a blind eye. Cornish juries showed complete partiality and threatened to render the law impotent. In 1824, for example, Mayor Bennet of Fowey was found to have £300 worth of contraband brandy in his house *after* he had thrown a good deal more into the harbour.

When Napoleon I tried to blockade the whole of Europe against

trade with England, it seemed – to those who knew how – almost a patriotic duty to run the blockade. The spirit of this Free Trade lasted into peacetime and the smugglers became known, almost as a term of respect, as Free Traders. The problem was beyond any effective local control. Recognizing this, the government gave the Navy the task at sea, and its officers took over the Revenue cutters. The Army was called in on land and the Inniskillings were sent to Truro.

The south-east coast of England may rival Cornwall as a centre of violent smuggling in the same period, but nowhere else has quite the appalling reputation for wrecking that has been accredited to Cornwall. It began as the normal seaside practice of beachcombing after a storm for some gleanings from the harvest of the sea, regardless of legal rights. In the early eighteenth century, the economic distress on the Scilly Isles made it a major source of livelihood. It could very quickly grow out of hand. Wreckers were easily tempted to neglect giving aid to drowning sailors, even to fight them for goods which they were salvaging. On occasion they helped them to drown, and this amounted to murder. In 1750 troops were sent to deal with the men of Breage and Germoe, renowned for their violence, who were plundering a damaged vessel which had come safely through storm and danger to the shelter of St. Michael's Mount.

Wrecking was undoubtedly a ghastly and barbaric practice, even if there seems to be no truth behind the fictional stories of ships being lured on to the rocks by false lights. There was much complaint among the locals when the first lighthouse was erected on the Lizard, since it threatened a valuable source of income. Perhaps the attitude is best summed up in the legendary prayer of Parson Troutbeck in Scilly: 'Dear God, we pray not that wrecks should happen, but if it be Thy will that they do, we pray Thee let them be to the benefit of Thy poor people of Scilly.'

CORNWALL UP IN ARMS

Curiously, the Cornish rebellions of the Tudor period had the effect of merging Cornwall with England more closely than even before. However, the cornish 'Entrance to England' was noisy.

Aristocratic Cornish families played an adequate part in the property spoliation that historians have called the Wars of the Roses. What is best remembered from this very lively period is the rivalry between the Edgcumbes and the Bodrugans. Piers Edgcumbe, chased through the woods of Cotehele by his pursuers, escaped them by throwing his hat on the Tamar, leaping in from a great height and swimming away underwater while his enemies riddled the hat with arrows, and thought him dead. Not to be outdone, Bodrugan, when the war had brought the wheel of fortune round, made a similar escape from his captors by jumping over a hundred-foot cliff to an islet where he was picked up by boat and carried off to continental exile.

Exceptional taxes can always make as good a reason as necessary for a rebellion. The Cornish in 1497 objected to the excess taxes demanded to pay for the war in Scotland which seemed to them to be of no immediate importance. The centre of the initial disturbance seems to have been St Keverne in the Lizard, where the blacksmith, Michael Joseph, became the first leader. Support grew rapidly throughout the county. At Bodmin a persuasive lawyer, Thomas Flamank, joined the leadership, and they began to march on London. At Wells they were joined by Lord Audley who provided a little 'tone'. The Kentish men were expected to join them, but, perhaps wisely, joined the other side. At Blackheath, the army of King Henry VII, which the offending taxes had helped prepare for the campaign against Scotland, dealt easily with the Cornish amateurs.

The rebellion was soon brutally over, but the ambitious Perkin Warbeck, pretender to the throne, saw his chance to start another. After a series of adventures, he arrived from Scotland via Ireland at Whitesand Bay near Land's End. At Bodmin he raised an army and set out for Exeter, where his attempted assault on the city failed. Perkin deserted by night when he heard the approach of the royal forces. Henry VII, coming to Taunton, pardoned the rank and file of the Cornish rebels. Perkin was captured at Beaulieu, Hampshire, and threw himself on the King's mercy, which was granted.

In the 1540s Henry VIII's war expenditure had forced him into financing the government by inflation – the Great Debasement. Prices rose sharply and, even more disastrously, the harvests were bad for three years in a row. These failures made an unfortunate beginning to the reign of the boy king Edward VI, who came to the throne in 1547. The Cornish complained of dearth to Protector Somerset, and he denounced their covetousness.

The other main source of extra finance for the government was from the sale of church property, and in 1547 it was enhanced by the suppression of guilds and chantries. The colleges at Glasney and Crantock were suppressed, although a few, such as St Endellion, managed to escape closure. While the Royal Commission surveyed all this extra property, including a mountain of superfluous parish church plate, William Body, the archdeacon who had almost caused a rising earlier in the year, took a lead in removing images in accordance with the government order. The men of St Keverne struck again and killed him, and a riot began which looked like developing into a Catholic rebellion, The Cornish gentry from further east quickly sent help and suppressed it.

In January 1549 an Act of Uniformity provided for the new, more Protestant English Prayer Book to be used – and none other – from Whit Sunday, 9 June. On Whit Monday at Sampford Courtenay in Devon the priest was compelled to say the old Mass in the old vestments. Meanwhile, in Cornwall, a rising was already taking place led by Catholic gentlemen. The Cornish appealed to the Protector for the old services because they 'understood no English' and because the new service was 'like a Christmas game', but that did not convince Somerset that they knew more Latin. He had received reports that in the boroughs men spoke more English than Cornish, and he seemed to think that the countrymen should follow suit.

At the same time, East Anglia was up in arms and proving very dangerous, but there appears to have been no serious attempt by them to link up with the Cornish, or vice versa. Instead the Cornish asked for a partial restoration of the monasteries and of half their property. When this was refused, the Cornish again marched east.

Most of the rebellion was fought out in Devon. The retreating Cornish made a late stand in entrenchments in Sampford Courtenay. As in East Anglia, mercenary troops were decisive. The period of 'pacification' which followed was even more barbarous than usual.

THE PERILS OF INDUSTRY

By the late sixteenth century technological advances were creating a great divide between the current generations of metal miners, who now were sinking shafts to forty or fifty fathoms, and the

medieval tin-streamers who worked the surfaces of the moors. Mining at such depths brought many new problems. Lack of air made it difficult to work more than a four-hour shift. To enable men to stay down longer meant constructing a second shaft for ventilation. This could be done, but it was an arduous and time-consuming task. In a deep shaft, wrote Carew, 'the workmen are let down and taken up in a stirrup by two men who wind the rope'.

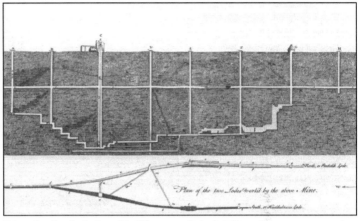

This section of a mine in the parish of Illogan, near Redruth, indicates the enormous amount of work needed to drive shafts and ways before most lodes could be approached. From an engraving in Borlase's *Natural History* (1757).

There was also the danger of flooding. Adits which sloped gently down to just above sea-level, or the lowest point which could conveniently take the discharge of water, made it possible to reach greater depths than previously. Sir William Godolphin, on whose land great mineral wealth was

Dolcoath Mine, Camborne. Seeing only ruined engine-houses today, we tend to ignore how much timber construction was also used to produce the headstock and winding gear, and the water launders (wooden chutes). From an engraving in *Views* (1832).

found, is usually credited with importing German experts to introduce the new techniques which they had learned in Saxony. One of these Germans, Ulrich Frosse, was much in demand in Britain. After finding copper at St Just, he went off to Keswick, and then on to South Wales where he ran a smelter at Aberdulais, near Neath.

Another problem was the possibility of bad ground. Carew says: 'Loose work is propped by frames of timberwork as they go, and yet now

and then falling down, either presseth the poor workmen to death, or stoppeth them from returning.' In solid rock they had to rely on axes and wedges to split the stone, and with the hardest of the granites this would slow progress virtually to a standstill.

In Lord de Dunstanville's revised edition of Carew's *Survey*, Tonkin's supplementary notes suggest that very hard rock was even more difficult to deal with by axe and wedge than Carew had suggested. Tonkin, writing in 1739, tells of the latest techniques for rock splitting: 'They formerly burnt furze, faggots, etc., to break the rocks; but that proving insufficient, and very often fatal to the workmen, by the sudden changing of the wind, which drove down the smoke upon them and suffocated them, they have of late had recourse to gunpowder by boring holes in them, in the nature of mining of towns besieged.'

This could hardly have sweetened the air, and bellows and lead pipes were needed to create a forced draught. Tonkin also describes the latest practice of covering the charge and train rather than boring a hole and tamping it in. This would in theory avoid the danger of sparks when tamping the powder with a rod, a practice which probably caused more accidents than any other during the next two centuries. Thomas Epsley of Breage, who is credited with being the first man to use gunpowder for blasting in a Cornish mine ('shooting rocks'), was dead and buried within twelve months. It is not difficult to guess how he died.

The advent of the Industrial Revolution brought steam-driven pumps to replace the old-fashioned water-wheels. A Newcomen engine was installed at Wheal Fortune in 1720, and at least three were operating in the county by 1741. Within twenty years or so, the best atmospheric engines could lift water from eighty fathoms. Improvements were still needed, however, to increase the power of the engines and to cut their enormous fuel costs. James Watt arrived in principle at the best solution in the same year, 1768, as the discovery of copper at Parys Mountain in Anglesey posed a new threat to copper mining in Cornwall.

The first trials of Watt's engine were a sensational success and Watt was able to obtain agreements whereby he was paid one-third of the value of the fuel saved in return for the use of his patented separate condenser. By 1783, when there were twenty Watt engines at work in Cornwall, the Cornish mine owners were objecting strongly to the amount they were paying to Watt, and a sordid period ensued, peppered with lawsuits as the mine owners were sued for evading their obligations.

The first half of the nineteenth century was the great period of prosperity for the Cornish copper mines. In the 1820s Gwennap parish alone produced more than a third of the world's output. New machinery was put to work in the booming industry, whereas tin

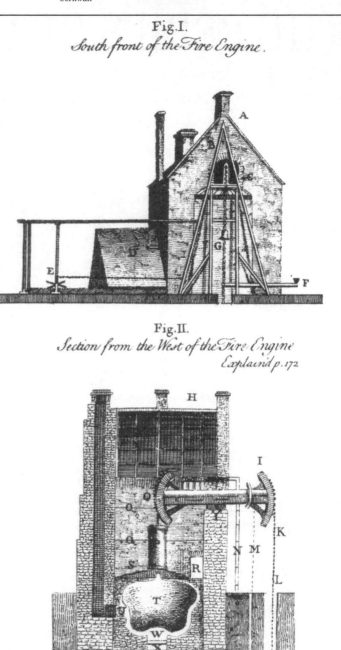

Fig.I.
South front of the Fire Engine.

Fig.II.
Section from the West of the Fire Engine
Explaind p.172

Above: These diagrams show an inefficient Newcomen steam engine before Watt transformed them with his separate condensers. The engine-house with the bob-wall, through which the rocking beam protrudes, was to remain a feature until the passing of steam.
From an engraving in Borlase's *Natural History* (1757).
Above right: Something of the richness of the Caradon mining area is shown by this map of 1845. Near the top left-hand corner, under the hill fort, its inner rampart looking more complete than today, is the Hurlers, the three stone circles pointing towards the barrow from which the Rillaton Cup was taken. Alongside is ground streamed for tin, the so-called 'Old Tin Dyke' which has been worked over and over throughout the ages. The rows of rings and ovals are shallow shafts left by 'old men' who long ago worked the backs of the lodes.

mining, the poor relation, had to make do with what it had. Railways with bullock traction, or inclines with stationary winding engines, or with locomotives, were planned and laid to transport copper ore. Par Harbour was developed to handle the ore and supplies for Fowey Consols, the second largest mine in Cornwall.

Not much of the prosperity seems to have got through to the working miners. In the early 1830s discontent and unrest spread from the agricultural workers to the copper miners. In the 'corn riot' of 1831 the miners of mid-Cornwall marched on Wadebridge and Padstow, using force to prevent the export of corn at a time of high prices. Miners in the St Blazey area struck against the tribute system by which pares (teams) of men bid against each other to force down the price for a job.

This was the period when Chilean copper production first seriously threatened Cornwall. In South America, Cornish capital, management skills and engineering know-how were being allied to cheap local labour to flood the market with low-priced ore. In the decade 1830 – 40 Chile's output was greater than Cornwall's, but by 1840 the first big discoveries in the Caradon area of south-east Cornwall gave hope to the home industry.

Free Trade was in the air, however. In 1838, the coinage was abolished. Five years later, import duties on foreign tin ores, although not on refined tin, were also abolished. Tin at that time was also under threat from cheap overseas sources, notably Java and Malaya.

The production of copper ore in Cornwall passed its peak in 1855–56, and thereafter it began almost to become a by-product of tin again. Invitations to Cornish engineers and miners brought large-scale emigration to South America. In 1866 came the great financial collapse. In four years the number of copper-producing mines in Cornwall

Pay-day at St Just Amalgamated Mine (in Penwith), 1873.

plummetted from 173 to 100. Some 7,300 miners emigrated in eighteen months. The air of dereliction which has not altogether vanished today began to hang over areas so recently buzzing with activity. More and more women with young families were left to cope alone, while the breadwinner went overseas to earn and send back what he could to support them. The average age of working miners in Cornwall went up; their strength and health went down. Conditions deteriorated in the mines themselves as the owners tried to survive by economizing on maintenance, with disastrous results. In 1869 at least ten antiquated boilers exploded. By the onset of the slump of 1874 only three substantial copper mines were operating, South Caradon, Marke Valley and Devon Great Consols, all in the eastern copper region. The prospects were grim indeed.

'Bal Maidens' was a generic term for all the women who worked at the surface of mines. These workers are at Dolcoath, Camborne, c.1890.

With mines closing all around them, some of the eastern miners tried to form a union in the face of the crash of 1866. They were locked-out, unemployed miners from the west were imported to replace them, and the union collapsed. Some 1,500 miners emigrated to the Scottish coalfields, and many more went to America and Australia; the total for that bleak period may have been as high as 5,000. The great Cornish Diaspora was indeed in full flow. Production of tin in old copper mines kept some work going, but there was none for the men whose mines had shut. The expansion of the china-clay industry and of quarrying helped some to find new jobs, but relatively few.

Even when there was work, conditions were often appalling. Many improvements were counterbalanced by new problems. Safety in blasting was improved by Beckford's Safety Fuse, introduced in 1831, and by the use of dynamite instead of black powder after 1860. But there was always some resistance to new, safer practices. The great advance of the 1870s, the powered rock-drill, almost immediately began to cause problems from dust. The death-rate of drill operators from chest disease rose to twice the average. Fortunately waterspray, which was also used to reduce dust after blasting, could deal with the problem – provided it was used properly.

One of the most serious strains on the men's hearts and lungs came from having to climb up ladder roads from great depths until the man-engine, or something better, was provided. Even then, the man-engine was itself a dangerous source of accidents. When the one at Levant collapsed in 1919, thirty-one were killed and twelve severely injured. Lack of proper underground sanitation produced epidemics of hookworm early in this century, a disease peculiar to such conditions. But the problem that Carew had written of in the early days of deep

mining, fatal roof falls, was still the most common cause of death underground.

The increasing difficulties of production at home, and competition from cheap labour regions abroad, have made the story of Cornish mining in the twentieth century one of a bitter struggle to survive. The two World Wars saw brief revivals, with subsidiary interests such as wolfram and arsenic in great demand for military use; these were followed by further prospects of collapse. At the time of writing, no-one can say more than that a modest future looks likely for the four mines now operating.

In the desperate days of Cornish mining earlier this century, the chief prospect for work for a skilled miner was in the gold mines of South Africa. One of my own Cornish cousins married a miner, and he had many a vivid tale to tell of how his father went out to South Africa to find work, while his mother, a good teetotal Methodist, ran a pub to keep the children until Father returned. He himself went out in due course, as did

Far left, top: Phoenix United Mine, near Minions, in the 1880s. The visible evidence of activity a hundred years ago has been replaced by dereliction and silence. The Count House, the old mine office seen on the right, remains a private house, but little can now be seen of the engine-houses.

Far left, centre: This photograph, taken in 1904, was posed because of the long exposure needed. The upper group of three men is using the old method of drilling, two men with sledgehammers alternately striking the head of a boring tool or 'boryer', which is held by the third man and given a quarter-turn between each blow. The man in white, below left, may be using a power drill. The photograph was taken at the Dolcoath 375 fathom level.

Far left, bottom: Blue Hills Mine, St Agnes, at the 66 fathom level, 1892–93. Timbering to hold the roof was already in use in Carew's day, in the late sixteenth century, but roof falls continued to be the greatest cause of fatal accidents in the mining industry.

Above left: One of the many old engine-houses near Minions. In many former mining districts these disused buildings dominate the landscape with their austere beauty.

Left: Headstock of Geevor Mine, a valiant survivor, largely saved by the efforts of Polish miners at the end of the Second World War.

virtually all the males of the family, and as he ticked his male relatives off with his fingers, it became appallingly clear that they had all died of 'the dust' in South Africa, or had returned to die of it in Cornwall.

John Wesley in Cornwall

The copper boom came so quickly to west Cornwall that it developed into a teeming, grossly overcrowded area at a much faster rate than the Church was able or prepared to cope with, and the standard of social welfare dropped. The miners lived in conditions of great uncertainty. Danger, disease, poverty and discomfort were part of the way of life. Occasional brief bouts of prosperity might allow the miner to submerge his troubles for a short while in alcohol. Uncertainty led to recklessness and violence. Smuggling and wrecking brought in useful extra income for some men, but their contempt for the law only brought more violence.

If there was little respect for the law among the eighteenth-century miners, there was probably much less for the Church. That was their mood when John Wesley came to Cornwall in 1743 to try and restore the Christian way of life. In a remarkable way he seized on some of the least pleasant features of the overcrowded settlements, the fears and despairs of their occupants, and turned them into opportunities. He freely used his understanding of crowds and crowd behaviour. Mass audiences, often in the open air in the early days, were moulded and stampeded by hymn-singing and emotional preaching, disturbed into violent experiences of conversion, the sudden gift of Grace following a dreadful conviction of sin. Under Wesley's guidance, ecstasy returned to religious life.

In the early years of his missions to Cornwall he met bitter, violent opposition. Partly this was because the Anglican clergy did not

preach in each other's parishes if not welcomed, and the wild scenes at Wesley's services were almost guaranteed to make him unwelcome. There seems also to have been a genuine suspicion, stirred up no doubt by his opponents, that he was a Jacobite agent. His *Journal* records moments of extreme physical danger in those early years, moments when

Billy Bray, the great local preacher and chapel builder who danced and sang wherever he went, taking religious ecstasy into everyday life.

he was only preserved by the magnificent courage that came from his faith.

Sudden conversion could easily be followed by relapse. To counter this, Wesley set about forming religious societies for purposes of mutual support. People joined these on a trial basis and then became full members with an appropriate ticket, renewable quarterly, and signed by the travelling preacher.

Many of the early meetings of Cornish societies took place in private cottages and houses. As the memberships grew, and money or labour became available, special preaching houses were built, called chapels at first and churches later. Probably the most famous of all the itinerant preachers, Billy Bray, who danced and sang his way about the county, was a great chapel builder. He worked, according to his inspiration, with his own hands, raising subscriptions, buying materials, preaching and dancing on the foundation stones. His first chapel was built on his mother's moorland field, using stones from the 'hedge' (Cornish for 'wall') as the main fabric. A number of these simple early chapels were built entirely by the hands of a

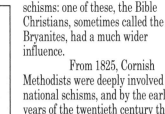

Above: Gwennap Pit, near Redruth. The engraving contains a rough version of a mine chimney behind the pit, Wesley's favourite preaching site in Cornwall.
Below: Crows-an-Wra. A substantially built Methodist chapel of finely dressed stone stands behind an early cross-head (see also page 31).

devoted group of men, perhaps just a father and son. With their simplicity of construction and shape, which they share with old mine buildings, they have an elemental quality which asserts the history of their society more bluntly than any medieval building.

Wesley made thirty-two visits to Cornwall. He was pelted with filth and abuse on his first coming, and fêted as though on a triumphal progress when he made his last journey. The final Cornish entry in his *Journal* shows what Cornwall had done for him: 'So there is a fair prospect in Cornwall, from Launceston to Land's End.' What he did for Cornwall is around us still.

The saying that schism begets schism could be aptly applied to the predicament of the Methodists after Wesley's death in 1791. It became impossible to hold the movement together, and between 1802 and 1841 Cornwall produced its own schisms: one of these, the Bible Christians, sometimes called the Bryanites, had a much wider influence.

From 1825, Cornish Methodists were deeply involved in national schisms, and by the early years of the twentieth century there were five denominations: Wesleyan, Bible Christians, United Methodist Free Churches, Methodist New Connexion, and Primitive Methodists. All had been chapel builders. Thus, in many Cornish villages, near the original Methodist chapel is another belonging to a breakaway group of Free Methodists. To this day, isolated chapels in remote places often turn out to be Bible Christian or Primitive Methodist foundations, which represented the evangelical wing of Methodism.

Since reunion, many such chapels have fallen out of use or been converted to fill some less spiritual gap in the community. One of the easiest conversions for a redundant chapel is to turn it into a place to store furniture or other bulky goods. One of the garages where I first took my car for servicing after the Second World War had been converted from a furniture store which had been converted from an old chapel. Twenty yards away, around the corner, was a Congregational church. This in turn was later closed and sold, but it was bought by the Assemblies of God, and so still fulfils something of its original purpose.

Across the river the United Methodist Chapel, near to its flourishing neighbour and not needed since reunion, is being demolished in stages. The Bible Christian Chapel in Wadebridge itself has been converted into a Youth Centre. Not all is lost. Perhaps the founders would have preferred the fate of Liskeard's Congregational Church, converted into a hall for the town's silver band, to that of Indian Queens', which became a restaurant, but they would surely have preferred this to demolition.

Decline of the Fishing Fleets

Whatever the motive, venturing in the seas off Cornwall was never an occupation for any but the toughest and most courageous, as the recent Penlee lifeboat disaster has reminded us. North of St Ives, the coast makes a long lee shore in prevailing winds. Padstow estuary is the only sizeable shelter, but it too can be difficult to make, and treacherous under many

conditions of wind and tide. Silting and sand-bars cause endless problems. One of the most touching pieces of writing from the pen of that great Cornishman, Claude Berry, describes how his great-uncle, Hodge Helbren, ferryman of the Black Rock Ferry, was lost on the Town Bar in sight of Padstow Quay. That ferry was one of the most ancient in Cornwall, and possibly had a Roman predecessor. The Doom Bar out in the estuary, which has accounted for innumerable ships, has its folklore

too. It is supposed to have been inflicted upon the town as a punishment after a Padstow sailor shot a mermaid with his cross-bow.

One of the most romantic of the tiny harbours is Port Quin, near Port Isaac. The approach from the sea is through a narrow cleft in the cliffs. On a dull calm day the walls of dark green and black rock are reflected in the oily water, and the atmosphere is eerie. When I first knew Port Quin its cottages were all in ruins. The story, as preserved in local tradition, tells

how the whole of the local fishing fleet was lost one night, and on the following day a ship reported steaming through the wreckage for hours with no sign of survivors. For a time, the women tried to carry on without the men, but in the end hunger forced them to give up the struggle and they went away. The village was abandoned, and even today only about four of the cottages have been restored; the rest lie untouched.

The coming of the railway to Cornwall brought new life, if only for a short time, to the Cornish fishing industry, by putting many of its ports in touch with the London market. The line to Penzance catered for Newlyn and Mousehole. St Ives acquired its own branch line, as did Looe with Liskeard. The lines to Padstow and Newquay tapped the north-coast fisheries. But by the end of the nineteenth century there were signs that the pilchard shoals were failing. Drifters and trawlers from up-country ports began to ruin the Cornish fishing grounds. French and other continental boats joined in. The two World Wars next took their toll, breaking the continuity provided by generations of fishing families. In the Depression of the 1930s many younger men went away. Boats which had decayed in the neglect of wartime were not rebuilt. Others, when there was no living to be had, were scrapped. What survives is different. The few remaining fishing vessels are outnumbered by the pleasure craft. The old fishing fleets have gone.

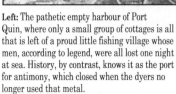

Left: The pathetic empty harbour of Port Quin, where only a small group of cottages is all that is left of a proud little fishing village whose men, according to legend, were all lost one night at sea. History, by contrast, knows it as the port for antimony, which closed when the dyers no longer used that metal.

Top: Its position on a tidal estuary at the first bridging-point of the River Camel, combined with the arrival of the railway, made Victorian Wadebridge a prosperous place. The single railway line, seen running across the road on the way to Padstow in this view c. 1882, has now completely gone,

Above: Calstock Quay on the River Tamar in 1907, when the East Cornwall Mineral Line still operated. This region enjoyed a lively trade in the nineteenth century with the booms in copper mining and granite quarrying.

THE CHINA CLAY INDUSTRY

The search for china clay in Europe began when local potters wished to produce fine porcelain, such as was being imported from the Far East, using local clays. But the secrets of porcelain manufacture were closely guarded, and there is a romantic legend of how Jesuit priests smuggled out specimens of china clay and china stone, transposing the labels, so that by accident we still call china clay 'kaolin', which is the Chinese name for china stone.

Early experiments in the South-West with local materials produced only soft paste, probably because talc was confused with china clay. Then in 1746 a Plymouth Quaker chemist, William Cookworthy, found china clay near Helston. China clay and china stone, equally important for porcelain, were found in nearby St Stephen-in-Brannel in 1748.

Beds of clay usually revealed themselves to prospectors on the moors as 'slads' (or 'sladdy bottoms'); these were waterlogged hollows, usually cut by very pure streams. The essence of the extraction process was to wash the clay into suspension in water as slurry, and then by alternately speeding up and checking the flow, to cause progressive precipitation, the heavier particles falling to the bottom first. At the end of this process, only the finest clay particles were left. This is the same principle as was used by the tin-streamers, except that the heaviest particles in the clay were waste, whereas with tin the reverse was true.

The first job when opening a pit was to clear the over-burden from above the pure white clay with pick and shovel. Then a stream was directed over the side of this pit in a wooden launder. Men in the pit helped the work of the stream in breaking up the clay and forming the slurry. This was then pumped from sand pits where the first unwanted element in the decomposed granite,

the quartz sand, dropped out. This sand was removed by shovel and horse and cart to the waste tips.

It used to be possible to distinguish the earlier of these famous Cornish landmarks at a glance. The nineteenth-century tips in the St Austell area all had flat tops where the sand was trammed out before tipping; later, tips were conical but nowadays sand is deposited by conveyor belt and the tips have become wedge-shaped.

The second unwanted element of the granite is mica, and this was removed by taking the slurry through mica drags and launders. The water then had to be removed by allowing the clay to sink to the bottom in settling pits. It was then dried by kiln; nowadays, this drying is mostly done by filterpress and the process is finished off in the Buell driers.

As early as 1791 Charles Rashleigh constructed the little port of Charleston on the south coast for the export of china clay. Horses and waggons used to take the finished clay in casks from the dries to the ports. These were later replaced by lorries and bags. Now much of the clay is pumped in slurry from the pits to the docks to be pressed and dried there, ready for loading by chute into the holds of the waiting ships.

On the whole, china-clay production prospered while the mines were in decline, but, perhaps surprisingly, mining employed far

more men for the same value of product, and so while the extra employment available in the china clay industry did something to alleviate unemployment in a small part of mid-Cornwall, that was the extent of the relief it could offer. And when the clay boom of the early 1870s broke, clay too ran into trouble. Sagging markets and falling prices produced attempts to cut wages, sparking strikes in 1875 and 1876–77. Although the year 1888 saw a peak in the value of clay produced, this was not passed until after the end of the century, by which time the quantity had increased by over fifty per cent. This, however, was just one aspect of the severe depression which overtook the county in the last quarter of the nineteenth century.

The end of a strike in 1913 was swiftly followed by offers of higher wages, but the days of hope ended all too soon with the coming of war which hit the industry hard. In 1918 the unions and employers worked together on the Joint Industrial Council, and after the Second World War the two sides of the industry set up a working party to explore its future. This group reported that china clay was now Cornwall's biggest export, not least in dollar markets. At the same time amalgamations and diversification were producing a stronger and better financial structure.

The astonishing expansion of the industry in recent years has

China clay near St Austell. The runnels down the surface of this sand burrow – quartz sand waste from china clay – betray it as no longer working.

come chiefly from the new uses that have been found for china clay. The biggest market for it today is in the manufacture of paper, for filling and coating. Well over half the material of many high-gloss papers is china clay. It is also used extensively in the traditional ceramic market and in paint, rubber and plastics, where a safe extender is required. Pure clay, even by itself, can be an effective stomach medicine. This is reassuring, since in a notorious case in 1814 at Truro it became clear that a certain Mr Potter had been using china clay for adulterating flour for two years!

It remains true that Cornish china clay seems safe from competition in markets where the highest-quality product is needed. Since the original granite was decomposed by forces from below the surface, there has been little staining and this has allowed a clay of unrivalled whiteness to be extracted. The other important quality, brightness, depends on the smallness of the size of the particles. A purification process is used to remove all but the very finest clay.

In this, as in the exploration of new uses for the product, there has been great scope for the application of new technology and scientific research. The principal firm in the industry has seized its opportunities eagerly. It was, for instance, one of the first industrial firms to buy and employ an electron microscope. New methods are continually being developed to keep the Cornish ahead of their competitors, and also to reduce the amount of hard labour which for so long characterized clay-work.

CORNWALL IN THE TWENTIETH CENTURY

If the now world-beating china-clay industry had to come through a time of trial in the late Victorian period before it attained its present eminence, other industries fared worse and had only moderate recovery. Few boats are now active in the ports where the large fleets once rode at anchor. Modern methods have enabled a little tin-mining to be re-established on a sound economic basis after almost complete extinction – a revival which was only possible in its early days with the help of Polish miners. The Second World War stimulated and revived Cornish farming, but it has always been a high-risk industry in Cornwall, never more so than with the threat of irrational changes in EEC regulations hanging like a sword of Damocles.

Economically, something has been salved from Cornwall's industrial past. China clay and tourism bring prospects of substantial growth in the future. Signs of all this are obvious enough to both native Cornish and visitor. The fishing ports are now chiefly valued for their picturesqueness and for the facilities they can offer the holidaymaker.

Many of the old fish cellars have been converted into shops, cafés and tourist accommodation. Instead of the departed pilchard, Cornwall must now receive and process an annual inflow of 3½ million summer visitors – a daunting quantity when set beside the county's resident population, a modest 400,000. The Cornish may complain of 'emmets' (ants) when

speaking of tourists, but the emmet industry is a cornerstone of future growth in the county.

On Goonhilly Downs in the Lizard, meanwhile, the landscape takes us to the edge of the future. There the great dish aerials of the satellite tracking station would make a fine setting for a science fiction drama.

The long wide inlets of the best south-coast harbours, and of Padstow, which was the only comparable one on the north coast, had needed ferries from the earliest times. King Harry Ferry, crossing the Fal River to Roseland, was the most beautiful of all. The picture on the left shows it in all its simplicity in about 1880. King Harry Ferry came into modern times, right, with chains and ramps that could be raised and lowered, and produced a collection of noises that could have come from nothing else.

Polperro, now a favourite village for visitors. In the old days wheeling gulls kept up a deafening screech as the boats unloaded whatever fish were in season.

ACKNOWLEDGMENTS

The publishers are grateful to Richard Muir who took most of the photographs.
Illustrations from William Borlase's Antiquities, Historical and Monumental, of the County of Cornwall (1769) and The Natural History of Cornwall (1757), also Views in Devonshire and Cornwall Vol I (1832) and Britannia Depicta, Cornwall (1813) were taken from copies kindly loaned by Michael Fleming from his personal collection.

Other illustrations were kindly provided by:
British Museum 20.
Cambridge University Collection of Air Photographs 38; 49 right; 53; 54; 71; 73 top.
Cornwall County Library, Local Studies Dept. 87 both.
Cornwall County Record Office 39 right; 79.
National Trust front cover top left, 21.
Newquay Publicity Committee 74 centre.
Ordnance Survey 40.
Royal Institution of Cornwall 25; 73 bottom; 74 bottom; 75; 80, photo by J. Moody; 81; 82 centre and bottom, photos by J.C. Burrow; 90 right; 90 left, photo by Herbert Hughes.

FURTHER READING

The archaeology and history of Cornwall has been written in a series of excellent books, and the foundation of it all is the delightfully written and keenly observed Survey of Cornwall (1601) by Richard Carew. The most useful edition is that by Lord de Dunstanville in 1811 which includes notes made by Richard Tonkin some three-quarters of a century before. The easiest version for access is included in Richard Carew of Antony (1953) by F.E. Halliday. From the same writer is A History of Cornwall (1959), a scrupulous but lively outline which synthesized work done up to the time of writing.

In 1954 W.G.V. Balchin's The Making of the English Landscape: Cornwall was published, applying some of the approaches of the greatest of all our historians of the English landscape, W.G. Hoskins, to Cornwall. The county is one of the richest in both archaeology and history. In 1932 H. O'Neill Hencken wrote The Archaeology of Cornwall and Scilly, a most remarkable book in its time. The picture has changed very much with subsequent work, especially that under the guidance of Professor Charles Thomas. His Gwithian: Ten Years' Work (1958), The proceedings of the West Cornwall Field Club, and its successor, Cornish Archaeology, have done much to make the new knowledge accessible. Susan Pearce's South West Britain brings together much of the recent work on Devon as well as Cornwall.

The tragic early death of Charles Henderson deprived us of what had promised to become his *magnum opus* on Cornish history. Instead we have the fragments, Essays in Cornish History (1935), reprinted by D. Bradford Barton whose press and pen have made an enormous contribution to the social history of the county, especially mining history, where he has continued the work of A.K. Hamilton Jenkin (The Cornish Miner) in a whole library of books published by his Truro Press.

Henderson's Essays give only an indication of the richness of the sources for medieval Cornish history, and recently John Hatcher has used a wealth of other material, mainly from Duchy sources, to produce the very scholarly Rural Economy and Society: The Duchy of Cornwall 1300–1500 (1970), and English Tin Production and Trade Before 1550 (1973). In the meantime L.E. Elliott-Binns had exploited the ecclesiastical sources on which his Medieval Cornwall (1955) was based.

In 1941 A.L. Rowse published a masterpiece, Tudor Cornwall, confirming the power already revealed in Richard Grenville (1937). Prodigious learning and research, building on Henderson's foundations, enabled this man of Tregonissey to take his place in the first rank of English historians with his early works on Cornwall.

Seventeenth-century Cornwall has been served well since 1933 with Mary Coate's Cornwall in the Great Civil War and Interregnum. The history of wars in which Cornwall was involved as a battlefield is not dealt with here, and the reader is recommended to Mary Coate's excellent work. Fortunately this too has been reprinted, in 1963 by Barton. The social and economic material for the period has been extensively worked by J.A. Whetter in Cornwall in the Seventeenth Century. John Rowe's Cornwall in the Age of the Industrial Revolution mined a rich vein proper to Cornwall, and provided the background into which the earlier phases of Bradford Barton's studies fit. In this period Cornwall was of special national importance spiritually as well as economically, and a fitting record of this has been supplied in the Rev. T. Shaw's A History of Cornish Methodism (1967).

For the traveller to Cornwall interested in its history, and for the native, probably one of the most important books is The Cornishman's House by V.M. and F.J. Chesher (1968). Peculiar Cornish housing fashions and developments from the Middle Ages onwards have been anatomized and pinned down by the two authors, and with their work in mind something of Cornwall's past can be read from the buildings of every hamlet, village and town.

Maps Finally, no explorer should go without the Ordnance Survey's Landranger (1:50,000) or Pathfinder (1:25,000) maps, or the special Outdoor Leisure map of the Isles of Scilly.

INDEX

Page numbers in italics refer to illustrations.